FEB 1 6

D0065932

popular

popular

The Ups and Downs of Online Dating
from the Most Popular Girl in New York City

Lauren Urasek with Laura Barcella

STERLING
New York

STERLING
New York

An Imprint of Sterling Publishing
1166 Avenue of the Americas
New York, NY 10036

© 2015 by Lauren Urasek

Endpaper photography by Emily Lambert.
Contributions from Kim Windyka, Lauren Reeves, Melody Rowell, Nikki Iscardia, Buffy, and Morgan.

ISBN 978-1-4549-1722-9

Distributed in Canada by Sterling Publishing
c/o Canadian Manda Group, 664 Annette Street
Toronto, Ontario, Canada M6S 2C8

For information about custom editions, special sales, and premium and corporate purchases, please contact Sterling Special Sales at 800-805-5489 or specialsales@sterlingpublishing.com.

Manufactured in the United States of America

2 4 6 8 10 9 7 5 3 1

www.sterlingpublishing.com

For all the girls who know.

Who the Hell Is Lauren Er-a-seck? Yer-az-sick? Oor-ay-sick?

I Lauren Urasek, (pronounced YER-AY-SICK) am NYC's most popular woman on OKCupid. When this title was given to me in January 2014, I was receiving, on average, more than thirty-five messages a day.

In just a few months alone, I received more than fifteen thousand four- and five-star ratings.

I rejoined OKCupid in January of 2014 after getting out of a short relationship that had initially started on the website. I quickly realized this second go-around might be a little different from the first. After only being back on the site for a few weeks, I was contacted by *New York* magazine. They told me I was the most messaged straight woman on the site citywide, and they wanted to write an article about it.

I'm a technology- and science-enthusiast-turned-makeup-artist in my twenties who spends my time studying astronomy, watching hockey, drinking whiskey, and working quite a lot. I've never claimed to be the hottest piece of ass out there, and having grown up as an ugly duckling, all my newfound attention came as a surprise.

It's flattering to receive the number of messages I did, but when it comes down to it, it's not the amount you receive, but the quality. I've gotten every type of message, ranging from "Hi, How are you?" to "My dick is hard with Satan's rage for your face." I actually deleted my initial OKC profile several days before I was contacted to be interviewed for the *New York* article. I made a new one in an attempt to lose some of the weird creepos who would message me day after day even though I did not respond.

Despite receiving gross missives like, "Sup freakshow? Wanna trade some naughty pics?" I still had hope that I could meet a great guy on the site. I haven't had much luck meeting guys while out and about in New York City; I've been told I'm intimidating and not that approachable. Maybe it's the tattoos and blunt haircut or the fact that my guard is always up. It's hard for me to even make eye contact with a stranger that I find attractive (something I'm working on). Still, in the age of the Internet, a lot of the guys I've come across seem to have very limited social skills. A lot of the men in this city are more concerned with their facial hair, freelance gigs, and selection of females than with forming a genuine relationship with one girl.

I met my last boyfriend on OKCupid, though, which gave me faith that I could do it again. But I am extremely selective about who I go on dates with, let alone message back. In the past three months, I've gone on less than five dates. The men I actually went out with didn't send any profoundly amazing messages (if those even exist). It comes down to "Am I attracted to him?" and "Do we have things in common?" If a guy's photos don't look like they're from 2001, we agree that religion is ridiculous, and he knows the difference between "your" and "you're," there's a good chance I'll respond. Seems simple enough, but in reality those few requirements don't leave me with a very large dating pool.

Out of the dates I have gone on, I've met guys that tried to kiss me within ten minutes of meeting me, told me about their background in porn, and propositioned me with monetary offers for sex. There was also the guy that treated me like a prospective employee for his very own imaginary "company of love." Instead of just having a normal, naturally flowing conversation, he launched into a manic Q&A session, telling me, "OK, let's play a game. You ask a question, then I ask a question." He started telling me about plans for children and the amazing house he had just bought, which would "perfectly suit me" if I decided to move in. When I realized we were on very different pages, I politely excused myself—but not before he desperately asked me what was "wrong" with him.

Then there was the time I thought the date was going rather well . . . until the dreamy, intelligent man in question decided to chug five glasses of whiskey in half an hour, leaving me with a really drunk dude who couldn't stop hurling into trash cans.

It's no secret that men in NYC have more dating options than women do, and they tend to avoid settling down until they're on their deathbeds. So it's hard determining who's genuine and who's not. Internet dating is exhausting and not very fun in the beginning stages. It can feel super-impersonal when you're comparing thousands of usernames and profile pictures, and trust me, the free oysters and bottomless glasses of bourbon aren't worth it.

Not every man I've chatted with has been skeezy or untruthful, though. There are also the guys I would have happily gone on a second or third date with who weren't interested in going on another date with me. Not even the most-messaged girl on OKCupid is immune to rejection.

I've been asked plenty of times why I'm the most-messaged girl. I don't know the answer to this. And I've received plenty of criticism for even trying to answer this question. If I said it was just my looks, I was bashed by trolls calling me fat and ugly or by people who called me a stuck-up, narcissistic bitch. If I said it was "brains," I was called ignorant and stupid because of course it's not brains, it's looks.

Here's my best attempt at an answer: It could be the tattoos, blue eyes, and correct spelling on my profile, or the fact that I don't write generic things like "I'm living my life to the fullest and I love long walks on the beach!" It could be that looking for a man isn't the most important thing going on in my life. (I think it's a problem when it is.) I'm confident and secure in who I am without having a partner. I have a strong opinion and know what I want. Maybe dudes like that? Or maybe they just have a fantasy of fucking a girl with tons of tattoos? I don't know. Whatever the reason, I'm not going to lie, it's pretty nice having my pick of the litter now, since I never did growing up. But still, attention from one thousand men doesn't compare in the slightest to getting attention from one man who really matters.

Reflecting on all the craziness of the past year, I feel lucky—and enlightened—in both positive and not-so-positive ways. Lucky because I know a lot of women who receive the same amount of attention I do online, yet on the particular week *New York* decided to take a data sample, I happened to come out at the top. It could have been anyone. I feel enlightened in a not-so-great way because, though initially I was entertained by the insane, inappropriate messages I received, now I realize that there's a larger problem at hand. The fact that it's so common for so many men to reveal their ickiest desires to a stranger—and, at that, seem to let go of all respect for another human being—is unsettling. On a positive note, though, accumulating a following that appreciates my blog has made me feel it's necessary to bring all this to light.

OKCupid may have hardened my heart in certain ways, but regardless, all the messaging and dating has helped me refine what I'm looking for, decide what I will and won't settle for, and made me feel more comfortable in who I am. It's helped me transcend some of my fears, insecurities, and neuroses—all while providing me with a hell of a lot of funny stories, bizarre anecdotes, and dating suggestions for whoever is willing to listen. Which is where you come in.

popular

The End That Led to the Beginning

I remember the last week of my longest relationship like it was yesterday.

I'd just arrived back in NYC after a long weekend in Maryland visiting family. At that time, I was in a four-year relationship with Christian, a pathological liar who also happened to be addicted to alcohol and several kinds of prescription drugs. I was very much in love with him, but looking back, I have to wonder what that love was based on. He was silly and made me laugh, but that's pretty much the only positive memory I have. The hard truth: I mainly wanted to fix him. It was a one-sided, emotionally destructive relationship in which I gave up my own passions and needs to take care of Christian.

We started dating when I was eighteen, and he served as an escape from under my parent's roof. We went on trips, moved to NYC together, got a cat, and shared deep secrets. Still, there was no "honeymoon" phase—there were problems from our very first date.

The week before I left for Maryland, we miraculously hadn't

fought at all, which, to my happiness-starved mind, translated into a faint hope that maybe we weren't irrevocably broken.

Walking into the empty apartment we shared, I put my suitcase down. "Hello?" I called out, kind of bummed but not surprised that Christian wasn't around to greet me. I texted to see where he was but didn't hear back. Sadly, it was a solid assumption that if he didn't respond, he wasn't sober and was most likely slurring his words somewhere nearby.

When you're in a relationship with an SO (significant other) who's constantly lying about every detail of his life, it can be hard—to say the least—to trust that person. And when I say lying about every detail, I mean seriously, *every fucking miniscule detail.* There was that time he blatantly fibbed about his grandma not sending a Christmas card; I later found the card hidden in our desk. When I casually asked him why he hadn't shown me, he got super-defensive and said he'd forgotten where he put it. Huh?

Oh, and there was that time he pretended he had a torn ACL (a common knee injury), going as far as to dramatically wrap his knee in an Ace bandage. There *was* no injury. And who can forget the time he lost his job but never told his family? Then, when they came to visit, his mom asked me if I was "going to Japan with Christian." Uh, that was the first I'd heard about a trip to Japan with the company he no longer worked for. I could go on and on.

Months beforehand, I'd given him an ultimatum: it was alcohol or me. This came after several sessions with a psychiatrist who bluntly suggested I break things off if Christian did not stay 100 percent sober. This wasn't the first time I had given him this ultimatum, but I'd never stuck to it because I was in a codependent place and just couldn't let go. When I got home from Maryland to find Christian MIA, it was clear that he was doing something he shouldn't be doing, so I rushed out to look for him.

When I stopped by a local hole-in-the-wall Austrian bar he frequented in Brooklyn, lo and behold—there he was, drinking at the bar and cozying up to a girl I'd never seen before. I felt the craziest rush of adrenaline overtake my body. Up until then, he'd done a lot of lame shit, but I never thought he would cheat on me. (If I could go back in time, I'd kick myself really fucking hard and probably punch him in the face.) Plus, he was breaking his sobriety. Christian in a drunken state was something I never wanted to deal with again . . . and now I had to.

Though I was consumed with rage, I tried to be rational. "Who is this chick?" I asked incredulously. When my questions were met by half-assed mumbling, I lost my cool and resorted to screaming. I turned to the girl and shouted, "DID YOU HAVE ANY IDEA THIS ASSHOLE IS AN ALCOHOLIC WITH A GIRLFRIEND?!"

"She's just a friend of a friend—no big deal," Christian valiantly attempted to explain. The girl scooted away from him at the bar and jumped in with a tepid "Hi, I'm Emilie," in a French accent. By then it was more than obvious what was going on. Even if he hadn't cheated yet, it looked pretty damn clear it would have happened that night if I hadn't walked in when I did.

I had no interest in prolonging our awkward conversation with twenty drunk hipsters watching, so I told him to come home with me (he didn't have anywhere else to sleep).

"You're drinking again, and I can't fucking believe you were with that girl. This relationship is over and done," I told him, my voice shaking, as we walked home. I also informed him that there was no way in hell he was coming on our planned vacation to Mexico later that week. He thought I was joking.

The next day, I woke up in bed alone; Christian was on the couch in the living room. Poking around on his social media accounts, like girls in unhealthy relationships do, I uncovered Facebook messages between Christian and the girl from the night before, Emilie.

Apparently she was visiting from France, and, surprise, she wasn't just a friend of a friend. She referred to him as her "American lover boy," and she had the nerve to call me a "psycho cunt" in one message. The best part? He'd agreed with her.

Christian's friends had always treated me like the crazy one in our relationship. Somehow they'd never picked up on his issues with lying or addiction—maybe because most of them were alcoholics, too. Christian tried to paint me as the bad guy when we argued, and somehow I often ended up believing him. This was just another example of that ongoing pattern. When I confronted him, he said, "She meant to send that to someone else." How fucking stupid do you think I am? Well, obviously stupid enough to waste years of my life with this asshole.

The rest of the week was a blur. Christian slept on the couch while I slept in our bed and avoided him as much as possible. I was still going to Mexico for a much-needed vacation that Saturday, and I asked my friend Alexandra to come in his place. I knew our relationship was over, but the fact that we had three months left on our lease made everything complicated.

That Friday, I took the train home around two o'clock. He'd left a voicemail and sent several texts while I was at work.

When I got to the apartment, I found a fifth of rum empty on the counter. He also seemed to have popped something like seven Ativans. (I discovered this when I sat down and found the almost-empty pill bottle lodged between the couch cushions). I already knew how he behaved on smaller doses of that drug— namely like a rude, mean zombie—so this was sure to be even more extreme.

In his delirious state, Christian started ranting about how "the biggest thing he's ever done for me" was . . . wait for it . . . *getting his ears pierced*. Yeah, it's as random as it sounds. Nope, I still don't understand, to this day, why he thought getting his ears pierced would be something that could save (or make any impact whatsoever on) our relationship.

In between awkwardly trying to hug me and falling face-first into the window blinds with his eyes half-open, he started yelling about wanting to go to Mexico with me the following day. Somehow I stayed serene; somehow, right then, I felt perfectly OK with the broken state of our relationship. It was the ridiculousness of the whole situation—plus understanding that his actions weren't my fault—that triggered this realization. I finally felt finished with Christian—for good.

When I went out for a walk to escape the domestic madness, my phone started blowing up. Christian called approximately fifty times in a row, then sent dozens of texts.

I didn't respond, but I did text our other roommate at work to warn him about Christian's current state of crazy. When I headed home after a few hours, I was dismayed to discover that Christian's scary stupor hadn't worn off. Instead, I found myself alone in our living room with a guy I hardly recognized—one who suddenly thought it was a great idea to chuck ceramic plates at my head. His whole ear-piercing stunt was bizarro, for sure, but this plate-throwing thing was . . . disturbing. It was the first time he'd ever intentionally tried to hurt me. (The first unintentional time was my twenty-first birthday in Vegas when, during one of our many Fights Heard Round the World, he had lodged my arm in a door, causing a massive black-and-blue bruise that covered the entire length of my bicep. Seriously, Past Lauren, I can't.)

I locked myself in our room and called the cops. When I warned him that the police were coming, he bailed—but not without punching a few holes in the wall, leaving behind bloody knuckle marks.

The only other occasion that I'd ever ratted him out like this was during a similar blowup (he drank a fifth of alcohol and swallowed a bunch of pills—you know, just your typical date night with an alcoholic). That specific time I was genuinely worried for his life. Several ambulances showed up, and he had to stay overnight in the hospital. When he woke up in the morning, he hated me for calling 911; he wouldn't speak to me for days. (What a horrible girlfriend I was for keeping him alive.)

When my roommate got home, we vowed to never let my now-ex-boyfriend back inside the apartment. I didn't cry—I might have even been happy. It felt like a switch had flipped in my head that day, and I finally felt free. I left for Mexico the next morning, but not without receiving another flood of texts from Christian proclaiming his love for me and how he would see me at the airport. I ignored them. He never showed at the airport.

Reflecting on it now, it's clear that I'd felt single for quite a while before breaking up with Christian. And even though we lived together, there was no sex, no love, no anything at all. Now that he was physically out of my life, I could truly focus on myself. Still, it's tough to go from a four-year committed relationship to total singledom. So after a month or so, I decided to try the online dating thing. I hadn't met anyone new in person, and I did everything else online—from ordering takeout to participating in every social network known to humankind—so why not try OKCupid?

In June 2013, I sat down at my computer and started writing a profile. I noted that I wasn't looking for anything serious, I was into guys with some sort of passion, I had a deep love for science, and I was an unrepentant grammar Nazi. In short, I was honest about who I was, and I tried to highlight some of my more unique qualities instead of just exclaiming, "I like to travel and make the most of every day!" I didn't overthink it, I just stayed honest.

I never dreamed that my simple, semi-un-noteworthy profile would attract as much attention as it did. I wasn't looking for that, and I definitely didn't expect it. But . . . it happened. And so began my official introduction to the weird, wide world of OKCupid, and my dating life—rather, my ENTIRE life—began to get pretty damn interesting.

Hung_and_Ready

Coming up with a half-decent username doesn't have to be a huge ordeal, but that doesn't mean you shouldn't put a little thought into it. Mine has changed several times with my love/hate (mostly hate) relationship with OKCupid, but most recently it was LoandtheCosmos. It's simple, but it reveals a little something about me.

Poke around on the site for three minutes and it's obvious: Not everyone knows how to come up with an online dating handle that passes the test of reason. And yeah, guys, this step *actually matters* if you want to, you know, find women who'll actually bother responding to you.

Here are some usernames you should avoid touching with a ten-foot pole:

BigBootyFan	DreamLovah
EnglishBoyin_bigapple	JewinNYC
ADangerousMan	WhiskeyBourbonBeer
Captain_HotStuff_4U	PussInBoots
SexAndCigarettes	SexyPants212
RumpShaker	ArtsyHipster
FriendANDLover	BUBBATHEBIKER
Christian-Grey	africanDream
BigBulge77	

THEY REALLY SAID THIS.
PART 1

When I saw your picture, I wanted to ask you out right away, but I was doing some hardcore training in my mountain-top dojo. I got too sweaty, slipped, and hit my head on one of my sex trophies. Klutz, party of me!! Anyway, while I wait for this nasty bruise to fade, perhaps we should hold off. What do you have going on this week?

Things to Never Ever Do on a First (or Second) Date*

1. Wear cowboy boots with American flags on them
2. Text me from the bathroom
3. Get in a screaming match with a cab driver, waiter, barista, or bartender
4. Ask me "where else" on my body I have tattoos
5. Be four inches shorter than you indicated on your OKCupid profile
6. Talk about your former career in porn
7. Talk about your ex-girlfriend *at all*
8. Refresh your Instagram feed the entire time
9. Drink four glasses of whiskey in thirty minutes
10. Call me your fiancée

* Yes, these are all real experiences I've had.

question. so —what on a man's body do you
think is the most fun part to caress and see
what the reaction is? aside from the obvious
places? and on a woman's body?

Standing outside a Capitals vs. Rangers game at Madison Square Garden on a rainy Sunday afternoon is something I'll never forget.

A few weeks earlier, on a first date with a guy named Dan, I'd mentioned how much I loved hockey, but that I hadn't had a chance to catch a game yet that season. Even though at the end of our date I knew I didn't want a second one, when he told me he would buy us tickets to a playoff game, I couldn't help but accept.

Yeah, it was a little weird that a guy I barely knew—who didn't even like hockey!—was buying my two-hundred-dollar ticket (some guys assume if they do as little as buy you dinner, you owe them a blowjob). But Dan didn't seem like the type to have an ulterior motive—just the opposite. He seemed alternately desperate and scared of me throughout our first date. His sheer niceness and eagerness to please were annoying, and I longed for him to be an asshole for just .2 seconds. *Just tell me I'm a bitch*, I thought. He would have wiped my ass if I'd asked him to. He was the type of dude who wanted everything to go *so* right *so* badly that he would apologize for *everything*. He'd even apologized when he started talking about chocolate and I told him I didn't like the stuff.

As if all my dreams were coming true, I got an unnecessarily long and, yes, apologetic text from Dan a few days before our hockey "date": "I am so sorry, Lauren. I've tried to rearrange my schedule, but it's just not working. I was looking forward to seeing you again and I'm so sorry that I won't be able to join you. I'll email you the game tickets and I hope you are able to get a friend to go with you. I'm so sorry." I was surprised he was cancelling, but not remotely shocked that his text was full of apologies. A wave of relief spilled over me.

I invited my friend Alison to come in his place. An avid hockey fan, she had been in Wisconsin visiting family that week but would be flying back into the city on the morning of the game. While waiting outside for her (and wearing a jersey for the opposing team, of course), I enjoyed the slurs the drunk bros were hurling at me, and by "enjoy" I mean abrasively laughing at how obnoxious excess testosterone can make men. I checked my phone repeatedly in an attempt to not feel lame. My excitement quickly turned to worry when I saw Alison walking toward me with tears rolling down her face.

"John's cheating on me. I found huge fucking elastic-waist denim capris on our bed when I got home from the airport," she told me.

I hugged her, but she said she couldn't stay, which I understood. I'd been in a similar situation with Christian less than a year earlier. Plus, not only did she find some other chick's pants on her bed, but she'd found *elastic-waist denim capris*. It's one thing to learn your boyfriend is cheating on you, but it's another when it's with someone who shops in the juniors' section at Kohl's and hasn't worked out a day in her life.

When Alison left, I called Mike, the personal trainer I was casually seeing, to ask if he could join. I figured nobody would pass up free playoff tickets. I was right, and he rushed over to meet me. I'm sure Dan wouldn't have been psyched to discover his two-hundred-dollar ticket went to a guy I'd already given blowjobs to, and I felt kind of bad, like maybe I should have just refused the tickets in the first place. But now here I was, at the playoffs with my extremely attractive six-foot-four babe of a date, and OK . . . I didn't feel *that* bad.

After the game, I ditched Mike and rushed home to get ready for my friend Caitlin's birthday party. I figured I would talk to Alison the next day instead of bombarding her with texts and calls asking how she was. I can't deal with girls who insist on pressuring friends to go out mere minutes after something shitty happens to them. I get it—you're trying to help them take their mind off things, but sometimes people just need to sit at home, cry, lose ten pounds from not eating, and pretend like the world is ending. If a few weeks go by and they still haven't showered or seen sunlight, then you have the right to invade their home and force them to put on a shirt that doesn't bear a lovely combination of tears and sweat stains. Until then, all you can do is be there for them if they want you.

Later that night, I headed to a bar in the East Village for Caitlin's birthday. I'd originally met the retro-glam-ish, red-haired Caitlin about a year prior, when I was in my ridiculously dysfunctional relationship with Christian. After we broke up, I had started hanging out more with Caitlin and a few other college friends of my best friend Kathleen.

Kathleen and I were, for the most part, always the only single ones in the group. Caitlin had gotten married to an awesome guy named Jarrod right around the time I met her. He got along with everyone and even put up with me asking him to take an unlimited stream of Instagram pictures of us when we were drunk. When all the couples around us were whispering sweet nothings in each other's ears, Kathleen and I were taking shots of tequila and making fun of them.

Tonight was no exception, and as I walked away from one group of lovebirds to Kathleen, who was grabbing a drink from the bar, I saw a familiar face out of the corner of my eye. I didn't have time to do a double take before Chaz, Kathleen's psycho ex, approached her.

Chaz had a long-standing history of being a complete asshole and making everyone around him detest him, and it seemed like no matter how often Kathleen tried to end their relationship, he kept reappearing. Not unlike my ex Christian, Chaz was an alcoholic with a pattern of lying and eternally painting himself as the victim. He even tried to fake his own death once, texting Kathleen and pretending to be his brother, saying Chaz had died. Then there was that time our good friend Val's parents kicked him out of their house for drinking all their alcohol and flirting with Val's grandma. (Keep in mind, this is a thirty-seven-year-old man.)

I don't know why I was surprised that Chaz showed up that night, but still, how the fuck had he even known Kathleen was there? They chatted for a minute before she ordered the supposedly dead person to leave, and, after that, everyone started to disperse and go home, including me, who was, by then, feeling annoyed with the guy issues my friends had to deal with that day. I was losing faith in the dude population by the minute.

I hadn't woken up that morning thinking I'd be granted two more examples of incredibly crappy men at my two best friends' expenses. All the rampant douchery my friends were dealing with made me think that maybe I *should* be giving nice guys, like hyper -apologetic Dan, a chance. Maybe it would have been fun for him to come to the game with me after all; maybe I'd judged him too harshly?

Luckily my trusty friend Google schooled me, bringing my cynicism right back to life. When I did a little Internet stalking, I was casually informed that Dan the Man actually had three kids and a wife at home . . . Of course.

Hey! How was your weekend, and how are you on this dandy evening? Engaging in any epic festivities? You seem like a really nice gal. My name's Gerard by the way. How are you enjoying this site? PS- your breasts are amazing

It's Not Just Me: Sarah, 34

The Carolinas in the summertime get incredibly hot and muggy, yet, inexplicably, you find yourself *wanting* to be outside. It was that magical feeling that lured me out to meet Alex, a man I'd encountered just hours earlier via Tinder.

Alex was cute and lanky and unshaved and weirdly enthusiastic about everything—the way stoners tend to be. I knew that he'd be sweet but scattered—and I'd be completely uninterested.

But it was something to do. "I'm going to the Pour House," I told Lisa, my cab driver.

"What the hell are you going there for?" She laughed.

"Why? What's with the Pour House?"

"I mean, you go to the Pour House if you like being around fuckups," said Lisa.

"This guy I'm talking to on Tinder suggested this place."

"What's his name?"

I told her. "We used to have a guy who worked for this company named Alex," she said.

I whipped out a photo and the driver's laughter confirmed it: Alex was once a part-time cab driver with the same company.

"He's a really weird guy," she said, eyeing me in the rearview mirror. "Nice—but you know, *really weird*."

I tried not to think about it, and a few minutes later, we

pulled up to a strip mall with the Pour House planted in the center.

Alex was at the bar, as he said he'd be, wearing a green T-shirt. His hair was a mop of curly tendrils, and, just as he promised, a Grateful Dead cover band wailed in the background.

"You look just like your pictures," said Alex, and I told him that the cab driver knew him and had called him weird.

"Thank you!" he cheered, and I laughed. He was heading out to Chicago for Lollapalooza in a couple of weeks. He liked the gypsy life, he admitted, and I was initially charmed. Though I felt absolutely zero sexual attraction to Alex, I missed a good Southern boy— that accent, their quirks and appreciation for the small things in life. So when Alex asked me if I wanted to ride back to his house and get stoned, I agreed.

"As long as you're not going to kill me," I told him. "Do you live in a high-rise?" I asked, fully expecting Alex to pull up at a clapboard house he shared with a hacky-sack player.

"Why, yes," Alex said. And minutes later we pulled up to a high-rise apartment building where a security guard lifted a gate to let us in.

"Wow," I said. My online dating psychic abilities were at an all-time low.

Once inside, I touched up my lip gloss and found Alex in his room, packing his bong. I proceeded to get stoned with Alex. So stoned, in fact, that I flew off into the Twilight Zone, and somehow Alex and I made out. "Look," I said, "I'm not going to have sex with you."

"Relax," he said, sitting up.

"Is this the part where you kill me?" I asked as he walked over to his desk and opened a drawer. His back was to me, so I couldn't see what he was looking for, but when he turned around, he was holding a gun. He tossed it to me, which I caught, then fumbled before realizing, *Holy shit, this is a firearm*.

I screamed and bolted for the door, Alex shouting, "It's just a BB gun!"

I turned to see him aiming the gun at his stomach and pulling the trigger. "It's not even loaded!" he shouted. "I'm so sorry," he said, putting his arms around me. "You were really scared."

I had to get away from this madman. While still very stoned, I remember Alex musing, "I live in a gated community." He said this with such profundity, as though he'd just realized how absurd his entire life was.

My cab arrived shortly thereafter.

Nerd in the closet or totally out?
A girl who can embrace her geeky side
is pretty hot to me. Forgive me for asking
(and, sorry, blame the 1:13 AM me) –

Submissive? Open to an older dom?

*Maybe you should take a chick
to dinner before you ask if she's
into being choked.*

. . . and Then He Punched Me

I t was a Tuesday morning in May, and I woke up feeling liberated. I had just quit a job I'd had for five years, and I had no clue what would come next. I'd been working for a well-known tech company that sucked me in with its amazing benefits and decent pay, but the monotony of the job had been making me miserable.

I'd made plans to meet up with a heavily tattooed and seemingly intelligent guy named Ethan that night. He had sent me a refreshingly respectable introductory message: "Hey, we seem to have a lot in common—I'd love to get together." He managed to bypass all my deal breakers: 1. He wasn't religious. 2. He didn't smoke. And 3. He knew the difference between "your" and "you're." In a nutshell, he looked attractive and he could compose a sentence. He got bonus points for being tattooed. With lots of tattoos myself, it can be hard to find a guy who understands the culture, isn't a moron, and doesn't see me as a novelty item.

By then, I'd been single for a good year and a half, but I embraced it—I was only twenty-two, so I wasn't necessarily looking for a serious relationship. I'd been casually seeing Mike for a few months. I liked him, but we were still dating other people. After all, he *was* twenty-five. In New York City, that's the equivalent of seventeen. Men in this city have way too many romantic options, and it can be hard letting your guard down when you know their eyes are perpetually wandering—you're never sure if a guy wants only you or if you're the tenth girl they've dated that month. Everyone says not to base current relationships on past ones, but it's hard to ignore the very familiar pattern that I and tons of other women experience all the time.

I wasn't in love with the trainer, but I had a sense of pride, like any woman, so the fact that he seemed more concerned about his deadbeat roommate's half of the rent than about *me* didn't exactly make me feel awesome.

My phone rang; it was the manager at a company I'd recently had two interviews with. Yay—she wanted to offer me the position! I texted my best friend Kathleen and told her we had reason to celebrate, so we decided to meet for margaritas after my date that night.

Around five o'clock, I text-confirmed with Ethan (you'd be surprised how many guys totally disappear instead of doing this). Waiting outside the restaurant where we were supposed to meet, I noted that it was one of those typical Lower East Side places that seemed to only offer kale, truffle oil, and bacon. When Ethan showed up, I was relieved to note that he (gasp) actually looked like his pictures.

We headed to a table on the roof, where I ordered a jalapeño margarita. As the waiter set the menu down, I noticed that Ethan's hands were shaking. Usually a guy being visibly nervous is a turn-off for me. Not because I think I'm better than anyone, but because my philosophy is: Why be intimidated by someone who's most likely also intimidated by you? Confidence is key—both my own and theirs—and to a find a man who exudes that is surprisingly hard.

Besides his nerves, though, Ethan had his shit together. He lived on his own in Manhattan and seemed really successful at his job. Plus, he paid for all my drinks without hesitation and he wasn't wearing plaid shorts or an Ed Hardy T-shirt.

Perhaps most importantly, he could hold up his end of a conversation. He talked at length about his work as a director, and though I occasionally felt like he was talking at me, not with me, I appreciated how our conversation kept flowing—there's nothing worse than awkward silences on a first date.

After an hour and a half of multiple drink rounds, I apologized and said I had to go. I felt awkward saying I had plans with a friend; I didn't want him to think I wanted to get the fuck out, but I also didn't want to leave Kathleen hanging alone at a bar.

As I walked to the subway, I wondered if I'd see him again. He seemed cool, but I wasn't totally sure if the spark was there. First dates can be unpredictable. There might be a physical attraction, but no one's let their guard down yet—not enough to let you see them for who they really are, anyway. Ethan and I had a lot in common, but I wished he'd opened up more, delved into his passions more deeply, instead of talking so much about work. Plus, I wasn't rejection-proof, and in the past I'd felt like I'd sparked with some guys, only to never hear from them again.

I hopped on the F train, which smelled, as usual, of homeless-man piss, to meet my friend at a margarita spot on the

Upper West Side. After we got a nice buzz going, we headed to Matchless, a Brooklyn bar that had a "two for Tuesdays" special. Something you should know about Kathleen and me: When we get together, spontaneity is the name of the game, especially if it's a weekday. One time, an expensive Italian dinner morphed into a trip to a super-trashy strip club in Bushwick. That was a Monday; I woke up Tuesday to find a bevy of strippers following me on Instagram.

Mike, the personal trainer I'd been seeing, texted and convinced me to head to his place after the bar because it was closer than my place at four in the morning. Then, between dancing to Beyoncé and dodging stray cigarette smoke, my date from a few hours earlier wrote me: "I had a good time, we should do it again."

I was taken aback, in a good way. In my experience, Most Popular Girl on OKCupid or not, NYC guys just . . . *don't do that*. Nope, it's usually a constant game of "which person is going to let their guard down first?" and if it's you, be careful, because nobody will want anything to do with you. I hate that game, so I was pleasantly surprised by his text. It made me feel special, which a guy hadn't managed to pull off in quite some time.

As I was contemplating my reply, the scene around me started getting crazy. Out of nowhere, I felt something hit the back of my head, hard. The guy to my right suddenly had a bloody nose, and Kathleen was looking into my eyes, asking if I was OK. Apparently I'd just gotten punched in the head (it had been meant for the idiot to my right).

The next morning, I woke up in the personal trainer's bed with a huge welt on the back of my head. It had certainly been an eventful Tuesday night! With a throbbing headache, I checked my phone, and pulled up the message I'd sent back to Ethan from the bar the night before.

After thinking it over, I'd decided that although first impressions are important, they're not *everything*, and nervousness be damned—you can really only determine how compatible you are with someone by getting more comfortable around them.

Meanwhile, the trainer was mad at me. Apparently my phone had died when I was on the way to his place at four, so he thought I'd been kidnapped by a crazed drug addict or something. I must admit, it felt kind of good knowing that he actually gave a shit, but, just like my sudden blow to the head the night before, it suddenly hit me that I had too much emotionally invested with Mike to not, you know, *be in an actual relationship* with him. We needed to either commit to something or end it completely. I chose the latter.

When I was putting on my shoes to leave, Ethan sent another cute message about something funny we'd discussed the night before. We texted throughout my whole bus ride home that morning. Our second date was looking more and more enticing, and it just served to emphasize the occasional beauty of online dating: the unpredictability of it all. Waking up the previous morning, I never would've guessed that later that night I'd get punched for the first time (a milestone!), not to mention that I would finally dump Mike after realizing I could and should hold out for someone, well, more interested in me.

Oh, and I'd had absolutely no clue that I would be meeting Ethan, the guy I would end up spending almost every day with for the next seven months—the one who would ultimately break my heart more intensely than anyone ever had before.

Hey do you really exist?

You are I think the most convincing case of existence of God A dumb monkey never can be evolved into you :-)

The grammar is destroying me.

Sugar

A Porsche pulled up outside my retail job on a Wednesday afternoon. I'd met John on OKCupid a week earlier and had been out with him once since then. I'd been surprised (but, uh, not THAT surprised—this is Internet dating) to discover that the guy who'd shown up to meet me wasn't exactly the guy I'd seen in his photos—it turned out he was around twenty years older than me. But at five foot ten with deep brown eyes, slick black hair, and an Armani suit, he was attractive and appealingly confident.

Over lunch at one of my favorite (previously special-occasion-only) restaurants, John vaguely mentioned that he was not only a doctor but a heart surgeon. Still, it seemed like he was leaving out details, and I had to ask a million follow-up questions to get anything out of him. While I didn't learn much about him during our first date, we talked in depth about the universe, psychology, and other mind-expanding topics. He had a way of making me open up without realizing it, and I was too curious not to accept his offer for a second date.

This time, I hopped in John's Porsche and asked where we were going. "The MoMA," he said. "Van Gogh's *Starry Night* is up. I've been dying to see it."

Paying thirty-five dollars to peek at one painting for two minutes seemed a little excessive to a girl who couldn't buy dinner the week before, but I'd realized by then that I wasn't paying. Plus, most guys' big date ideas don't seem to extend much beyond "getting drinks," so it was refreshing being with someone who had even the slightest inclination to go to a museum in the middle of the week.

After looking at the famous painting for no longer than I would've brushed my teeth, we stopped in the gift shop on our way out. I flipped through some books, and it seemed like every other one I picked up, he had already read. John's intelligence and presence actually made me feel pretty insecure—and though I was out of my comfort zone, I felt it might be a good thing.

He picked out several books without saying anything, brought them to the register, shelled out more than two hundred dollars, and handed me the bag. "You want me to hold these?" I asked, confused.

"No, they're yours."

Though my last boyfriend, who I'd been with for four years, wouldn't even buy me a turkey sandwich from the bodega, since then I'd met various men who asked if they could "spoil me"—take me shopping or buy me expensive meals. It isn't that uncommon in New York, and to a broke, single girl, it always sounded pretty damn good, though I never took anyone up on it. I'd read some blogs by women in the sugar-daddy world, and despite what the media might have you think, their experiences sounded, well, hard. It's something that's totally frowned upon by society (for the women, at least—double standards at their finest!).

Anyway, that whole sugar-daddy thing was what came to mind after my first date with John. He was leading with his money, trying to impress me with material things. He didn't just pick me up in his Porsche but also felt the need to talk about the model and specifications. He would always throw unnecessary little details into his conversations, like the price of a ticket to an event or how much his shoes cost. It would have been annoying if that was all he ever talked about, but he balanced it by being one of the most intelligent people I'd ever met. It almost seemed like he wasn't being genuine, or he was only trying to impress me because he knew I was too young for him.

Over lunch at the museum restaurant, I ordered something I couldn't pronounce and an obnoxious dessert that looked like an architect had built it. John started telling me about his upcoming trip to LA, where he'd be speaking at a conference for hundreds of doctors. I jokingly said I wished I could go. It was a typical make-you-want-to-kill-yourself winter in NYC, after all. He quickly responded, "Get off work and come with me." I didn't think he was serious, so I laughed it off.

When the bill came, I couldn't help but be curious—oh, just two hundred dollars for the two of us and less food than you would have gotten for two dollars at McDonalds. At this point it was only about four o'clock, and he insisted on showing me one of his favorite stores in SoHo, so we jumped in his car and headed downtown.

We spent the late afternoon walking around, and I could feel people dissecting us with their eyes, trying to figure out what our deal was. It made me feel like I was doing something wrong, and I hoped I wouldn't bump into anyone I knew. I tried to ignore the stares and focus on our conversation. The passion he felt for helping people who needed life-saving surgeries and didn't have money or insurance was inspiring, and I picked his brain as much as I could.

We went to his favorite store, where he bought me a brown leather bag that I still use to this day, before finally driving me home. Though I knew we weren't destined for, like, a passionate long-term love affair, I believe meeting people who change your perspective is always a good thing. Though I probably won't be performing heart surgery anytime soon, it's interesting to learn about something you otherwise wouldn't have.

John texted a couple days later and asked if I was serious about going to LA. I immediately responded, "Of course, but are YOU?" He told me to use his credit card to book a flight, which I did. I immediately went from "Should I trust this dude?" to "Um, he's pretty naive." What's stopping me from buying a Saint Laurent bag or ordering way too much shit on Amazon? I mean, I wouldn't—I'm a nice person—but he didn't know that.

I know some people might have thought I was an idiot for agreeing to that trip. I think spontaneity keeps life exciting, though, and as long as he wasn't a serial killer or wearing Crocs, I'd survive. Plus, I had control over my flight reservation, I insisted on my own hotel room, and it was only three nights.

It was about a week before our trip that John and I met up for the third time. He took me to a cozy restaurant that served the most amazing sushi I'd ever had. We continued our previous conversations about cosmic theories and sipped some sake. With a nice buzz going, we headed to the Comedy Cellar. We still got looks when we were out together. Besides the age difference, a typical pretty girl with tattoos and black hair wouldn't normally be seen with the type of man John was. I never said I was typical, though.

Sitting in the front row of a comedy club on a date with someone you've known only for a few weeks is kind of the worst possible situation—well, besides puppies ceasing to exist. At this particular club, the comic is literally two feet in front of you, and it's so tightly packed, you can feel the breath of the girl sitting behind you. I took a sip of my drink and made eye contact with the dude onstage. He immediately bellowed, "What the hell is *this* girl doing with *that* guy?" One hundred fifty people burst out laughing, and I could tell John was extremely uncomfortable, though he tried to play it off by awkwardly joining in the laughter. In that moment, I realized that these kinds of men are *not* the ones in the power position. They are literally paying for good company, and while I did genuinely enjoy our conversations, if I wasn't being wooed by the free shit and lavish lifestyle, I wouldn't be out with him, and he knew it.

We hopped in a cab. Up until then, we hadn't had any kind of physical contact aside from a hug. I actually kind of forgot I was "dating" him; I saw him more as a friend. Maybe it was the few drinks he'd had or the fact that I had been seeing him for a few weeks and hadn't even kissed him, but he started tugging at my sweater while trying to pull me closer. My first thought: *This is a brand new sweater and you're gonna fuck it up, dude.* My second thought: *This is super-uncomfortable and not at all what I want.*

I pulled away and politely said I was tired and had to head

home. He respectfully agreed and told the cab to drop him off first. Right before John stepped out, he mentioned that he'd forgotten to give me something. Then he handed me a white envelope, smiled and shut the door behind him. When I opened it, I found several crisp hundred-dollar bills—and by several, I mean twenty. Holding two thousand dollars cash in your hand when just weeks earlier you couldn't buy ramen noodles is a high I don't know if I'll ever experience again. All I could think about was getting more money.

Without any context, if I'd just told you an older man handed me two thousand dollars in cash, you'd automatically assume I'd fucked him, and I wouldn't blame you for coming to that conclusion. Why would someone hand over that much money to someone for just going to dinner with him? I asked myself that same question. Did he *expect* me to fuck him the next time I saw him?

Still, I became more intrigued by John. Right when I got home, I did some Googling to find the staff page of the hospital he worked for. Guys should know that females are the ultimate spies and will adeptly uncover anything you're lying about. So, there "John" was on the hospital site, photo and all . . . but his name wasn't John, it was Elliot. I continued my Google-stalk session and uncovered his home address in upstate New York, as well as the names of his wife and, yes, two children. He'd mentioned none of that stuff before.

I told Elliot what I'd found, and that I would no longer be going to LA with him. He gave me a simple "OK," and that was the last I heard from him.

For almost a year after that, feeling addicted to the lifestyle and enjoying being single, I continued exploring the forbidden "sugar relationship" world. I met some amazing and not-so-amazing people and went out with some of the wealthiest guys in the country. Despite the fact that I wouldn't sleep with any of them (yes, really), I was given cash, bags, shoes, clothes, and endless dinners and drinks.

At first I was secretive about the few dates I had gone on. Then I felt the need to share some of my stories with friends. Most were extremely intrigued and couldn't stop asking questions; some even decided to give it a shot themselves, quickly learning it wasn't as easy as it seemed.

Sharing this here was something I struggled with, because as we all know, our culture scorns anything even *slightly* resembling sex work. Still, I'll defend my choices to this day. If you knew how common it was for twenty-something women to do exactly the same thing I did, maybe it wouldn't be so taboo. And maybe we women wouldn't be labeled "whores" and "sluts" while dudes get praised and high-fived for all their free-wheeling ways.

In any case, I learned a lot from my brief pseudo-"sugar-baby" experience. You can have all the material shit you'd possibly want, but if you're not happy with the company you keep, you'll be miserable. I finally stopped because I didn't actually like any of them. Plus, I realized a luxurious but empty lifestyle can get really old really fast.

Although being handed two thousand in cash seems like easy money, the relationships I had weren't real. It was about being the perfect company for a guy who probably had a lot of shit going on that I didn't know about and acting like I was genuinely into him. I had to put my own problems on hold to be the perfect date who always dressed to impress and never showed up without a fresh manicure. Now it's much more satisfying making my own money and saving my time for guys I actually feel something for. Or ones I *might* feel something for . . . as long as they don't own any Crocs.

It's Not Just Me: Louisa, 32

I've been Internet dating on and off since 1999 (yes, humiliating), back in the days when people didn't even post photos with their profiles. It was the Internet-dating dark ages, pretty much literally. Today isn't much better, of course. There's never a guarantee that the guy (or girl) who shows up for your date will look even kind of similar to the person in their pictures, a lesson I learned the hard way—for the millionth time—when a guy showed up for our Tinder date with his TWO FRONT TEETH missing.

Mark seemed like a cool enough guy from his profile. Brown hair, blue eyes, mid-thirties, good job at a major university in my city. He described himself—and what he was looking for—like this: "Grown-up (ish), indie/punk/hipster professional dude, in search of forever and/or fun."

I liked the "forever and/or fun" thing. I thought it was clever and it made perfect sense. I was looking for the same thing, depending. I mean, I could deal with something casual, but something more serious and long-lasting would be even better.

He suggested we meet for dinner, which I usually don't do, because dinners can stretch on for hours and who wants to waste hours on someone they don't even know? Somehow he convinced me, though. When I saw him approaching the restaurant, I realized my initial dinner-less instinct had been dead-on. I fought the urge to bolt as he offered an awkward little half-smile, and said "Hey, Louisa? Good to meet you."

Whoa. A big, black, gaping hole was staring out at me from where his two top front teeth should be. Why the hell did this schmuck think it was normal, or even APPROPRIATE, to be, like, out there going on Tinder dates like nothing was wrong? Did he really think he was hot enough for that? (He most definitely wasn't.) More importantly, did he really think women wouldn't care about something like . . . missing teeth? I mean, I know the dating scene is rough in major cities, but come on, most women I know aren't THAT desperate.

Regardless, I didn't flee—I didn't want to be rude—but I tried to keep the ensuing dinner as brief as possible. He wasn't a bad guy, as it turned out. Our conversation was reasonably good, and I might even have wanted to go out with him again if it weren't for the teeth thing, which he said was the result of a bike accident. He hadn't gotten them fixed yet because he was getting dental implants instead of regular-person crowns. Dental implants, if you're not in the know, are fake teeth, basically, that are expensive as shit and take up to a YEAR to put in your mouth. Yes, this means dude would be walking around toothless for a YEAR.

Things got even stranger when he casually mentioned that he was about to take down all his online dating accounts down because "he'd met a few really cool girls he wanted to get to know better."

"Oh, playing the field, huh? Doing a little juggling?" I asked bitchily. I was annoyed—I thought it was a pretty much a universally understood faux pas to talk about other chicks you're dating on a FIRST DATE. No matter whom you're out with or how well it's going.

"Well, yeah, kind of!" He admitted with a gross little grin. CHECK, PLEASE. Suffice it to say, we never spoke again, but good luck to Mark and his supposed gaggle of Tinder chicks who apparently have no standards.

Hey, how's it hanging? Altho I dont want to sound conceited by any means,I think honestly that a girl like you deserve good-looking, educated , successful professional guy like me but if you are in to losers like every other guy (will messaged you before me and will do after me)on here than please ignore my message else will take it forward when respond to me . Lol ok . Hey your beautiful and I am not that of a jerk but whatever I said about you and me is kind a true. Look forward to talk to you.

You're single because you have an oversized ego and you can't write a paragraph properly. You are not actually as good-looking as you think you are.

The "F-Word"

Feminism: *The advocacy of women's rights on the grounds of political, social, and economic equality to men.*

There's no word as misrepresented and misunderstood as "feminism." It's 2015, but tons of women still seem resistant to associate themselves with either the label or the movement. I guess it's because they're scared of being seen as man-hating lesbians with hairy armpits, or maybe they just don't know what the word actually means.

If you believe every gender should have equal rights then congratulations, you are a feminist, my friend. And if you have a penis and still manage to believe that everyone should have equal rights, you're also a feminist.

For me, beyond the basic definition, feminism is about women owning our lives. That means doing what we want, what makes us feel good, and—preferably—what's helpful to other women, whether that means running your own business that employs other ladies or supporting females instead of tearing them down. In my world, feminism also includes speaking candidly about who we are and how we feel. Which is part of why I launched my blog—and why I wanted to write this book.

Remember the "Not All Men" Internet sensation that struck last year, where loads of dudes valiantly tried to prove they were exceptions to the sexist rule? On my blog, I responded to tons of messages from guys trying to defend themselves for (supposedly) not being your usual offensive asshole. I get it. You may not have killed a girl because she didn't have sex with you, but I bet you *have* judged her for the amount of sex she's had or the degree of cleavage she's bared on a Saturday night (even as you gaped longingly at it from across the bar).

One of the first steps to gender equality is, IMHO, to admit you can't ever *fully* put yourself in someone else's shoes. If you don't have a vagina, sometimes you need to learn when not to speak—not because what you say doesn't matter, but because, well, you don't have a vagina, so you will never fully get it. Instead, try supporting what women say and trusting that what we feel is valid. All your desperate attempts to prove you're not like the rest of men feel fake. Instead of making it about you, how about listening and acknowledging that rape, slut-shaming, and attacks on reproductive rights are actual *issues,* and that women who talk about them aren't just ranting feminazis?

Exposing the outlandish messages I've received from guys on my blog started off as a joke, but honestly, "Can I eat Nutella off of you?" as an opening line is just too good to keep to myself. Thus, my Tumblr, They Really Said This, was born. I didn't necessarily have some grand intention or deep thought behind it until the messages started piling up, people started freaking out about them, and I realized how gross what these guys were saying actually was. By exposing them I wanted to help showcase all those fine gentlemen of our generation who still see women as objects. Receiving messages from guys who wanted to "see my titties" without even asking my name clearly shows 1. their level of intelligence, and 2. their lack of respect for women.

I never realized how much of an impact my blog would make or how it would inspire, comfort, and even anger men and women alike. What makes it worth it for me is the reposts and notes I receive from followers who appreciate it as an outlet. It shows I'm not the only one experiencing these things—in fact, it happens to all women. I've had emails that range from a fifteen-year-old girl in Oklahoma thanking me for my confidence, which inspired her to stand on her own when previously she had lived only to please boys, to an email from a father thanking me for being a positive role model for his daughter. My goal is to empower girls and women to take control over their bodies, lives, and success. At the same time, if I can create awareness that this is a universal problem, and good people who believe in equality acknowledge that, maybe the crude objectifying messages will pop up in our in-boxes less often.

Those messages seem like a small issue compared to the massive real-world problems of sexism, rape culture, and inequality, though. Whether it was a week ago when I was walking home and a guy decided to yell at me, "YO, MA, YOU KNOW YOUR PUSSY SO WET!" or that time I was shoved in a room in high school and would have been raped if I hadn't kicked the dude in the face, every female has stories. Countless stories. I consciously decide what street to walk down every day in order to get catcalled less, and if I am dating someone, I consciously try to hold out on having sex, even though I want to have it, in order to not be seen as a whore. We are expected to marry and have kids by a certain age, and if we decide that isn't the best path for us, we are seen as damaged. However, my experiences mean almost nothing compared to the women in Saudi Arabia who get raped and forced to marry their attackers, or the fact that 51 percent of women in Pakistan are illiterate, compared to only 18 percent of men.

Some of you might read this book and think of me as a slut, whore, or another lovely nickname for daring to share my rich (and often ridiculous) array of dating experiences with the world. That's your call, but my life is not *that* interesting, and it angers me that while men can run around half-naked and get high-fived by idiotic bros for the amount of ladies they fuck, women are perpetually shamed for the decisions we make about our own bodies (not to mention the enraging fact that we're generally presented with only dumb, pink crap with stupid slogans on it—"love," "peace," etc.— at the stores that supposedly cater to us). I will never understand why anyone would bother pointing fingers at me for my drunk one-night-stand or the low-cut shirt I wore last week.

Still, I had to make a deliberate choice to share all these experiences with the world, and it's ironic that, even as a feminist, I paused before doing that because I was scared of how society might view me. This just proves to me how far we still have to go and how important it is for women to keep talking about their own experiences, both online and off.

Blue is for Boys, and Pink, Glittery Everything Is for Girls

As a kid, walking into a toy store and seeing the obvious divide between pink and blue was an easy way to spot which toys were for GIRLS and which ones I would supposedly have no interest in—because they were for BOYS ONLY. Gender-specific products are why I had to go to multiple stores to find black boxing hand wraps that fit me and why my nephew wouldn't use my niece's pink plastic bow and arrow. I don't know who decided I'd like only pink things or that guys need to hand in their man-card if they decided to forgo the blue stuff, but it needs to end. I've compiled a list of some of my favorite gender-specific products for your enjoyment.

❶ Bic pens "for her." THANK GOD there is now a pen made just for my dainty, little hands that I can write love letters with to the boy who will just, like, never even notice me.

❷ Men's vs. women's razors. I'm so happy I don't have to use those ugly black razors to shave my legs. Oops, did I say I shave my legs? I mean, my legs are actually always naturally smooth because society wouldn't accept me if they weren't.

❸ Baby carriages (in pink) and fake babies. Better get 'em started early! These girls will need to know how to raise a child, because females are useless if they're not utilizing their motherly instincts.

❹ Sleep Pretty in Pink ear plugs. One time, I tried to use blue ear plugs when a man was using his loud, manly voice to tell me how to dress, but they just weren't effective. Luckily, they came out with a version just for me!

❺ Rhinestone-encrusted sports jerseys. I just love that I'm able to buy a cute, sparkly, and fitted jersey (to show off all my curves, of course) that I can wear to the game I know absolutely nothing about because the rules are just way too complicated for ladies!

THEY REALLY SAID THIS.
PART 7

My dick is hard with satan's rage for your face!

Wait, what?

Being happily single means loving my life for what I've done and who I am. It means not succumbing to the idea that our culture has instilled about "having issues" if you're not in a relationship. It means eating unhealthy amounts of Ben & Jerry's and not having to tell anyone when you're going for last-minute drinks with your best friend or just walking to the liquor store to buy a bottle of wine. It means being able to go out after work and not worry about whether you get home at 5:00 PM or 5:00 AM. It means not giving a fuck how your hair looks when you wake up or if last night's mascara is on your chin. Being single is the absolute freedom to talk to whoever you want, flirt with whoever you want, and fuck whoever you want. I have been the most content I've ever been in my life when I'm single, because I know my happiness is dependent on nobody but me.

I wasn't always at this point, and I don't think being single is easy for everyone. I've definitely been in a few shitty relationships that I refused to end because I didn't want to be alone again. Two of my ex-boyfriends were clearly cheating on me, but I swept the clues to the back of my brain because I felt it would be too "inconvenient" to be on my own. It seemed almost impossible to have to move out of the apartment I shared with my ex or cancel the upcoming vacation we had planned together. And sure, before finally realizing how great singledom can truly be, I may have drunk-texted an ex or two sounding desperate as fuck—but no longer. The owner of a penis will not determine my happiness; I will.

People have given me crap about why I'm on an online dating site if I'm so thrilled about being on my own. But for me it feels perfectly normal to want someone to go on trips with and have conversations with about the crazy homeless dude I just encountered on the street. That doesn't mean a partner is *required* in my life. It just means it's natural to want to share experiences with someone you love.

Anyone who says they need a significant other to feel complete is too scared to admit there's other shit going on internally that they just don't want to deal with. You can't expect a relationship to go right when you're starting off miserable in a shitty job or freaking out about the ten pounds you gained recently. Getting into a relationship or continuing a bad one just because you're lonely is dangerous, and it usually leads to fucking misery.

I broke up with my ex-boyfriend Christian about a year and a half after we'd moved to New York together. Though my sanity was entirely missing in action for the four years we were together, I fucking held on. I'm sure everyone looking at us from the outside thought we were psycho. I never trusted him, and he lied twenty-four hours a day. Plus, he failed to pay his half of the rent, and our roommates despised us, because, duh, living with a constantly fighting couple is probably even worse than an obnoxious teased-hair chick from Long Island who still wears UGGs. I would have HATED Lauren Urasek circa 2010. The thing that made me finally break up with him was the absurdity of it all, and some super-dramatic shit he pulled in the haze of addiction (check out "The End That Led to the Beginning" on page 3 for more details on our downfall).

When I broke up with him, I was single for the first time in years, and it felt . . . weird. I joined OKCupid a month later, idiotically thinking I was stable enough to sustain something new. Someone that fresh out of a relationship should *not* be seriously dating. All I should have been doing was looking for fun, dumb rebound after rebound, but instead I felt a void I needed to fill.

Moving to a new apartment on my own was a shock to say the least. Sleeping in a bed by yourself and not having anyone to greet you when you come home after years of being accustomed to that it is, well, lonely. I didn't even miss Christian, I just missed the idea of him. As the months passed, I didn't date anyone seriously, but I did manage to get comfortable dating casually and focusing on myself—probably the most important thing I've ever done.

Becoming comfortable with being alone has been totally empowering. If I actually *had* found someone to date so recently after that breakup or, worse, if I'd wound up getting back with my ex, I wouldn't have discovered how ABSOLUTELY FUCKING AWESOME it is to not rely on anyone else for your happiness, sanity, success, or mental health. I've traveled to other countries by myself, gone to dinner by myself, and have done countless other activities alone, and I don't feel the need to apologize for it or feel even slightly awkward about it.

I will never feel bad about being single again, and if I do eventually find someone to share my life with, it'll be because they inspire me to be a better person, not because they "complete" me. I'm a whole person all on my own, thanks very much.

Last night I had a dream that a grilled cheese sandwich was eating me. What do you think that means?

Any suggestions for this guy?

A Note for Dick-Pic Enthusiasts

Hey guys! So, real talk: No girl wants to see your penis. The worldwide female committee never got together and voted on wanting to see your dick pictures. We're still on the fence about whether penises are even attractive body parts to begin with.

Before digital cameras, a guy would have never gotten a photo of his penis developed at the grocery store—and if he did, he would have been publicly mocked and shunned as a major creep. Yeah, yeah, I understand how proud you are of this beloved body part you all possess, that you're just DYING to show it off. But, it's ugly. The only time a dick pic is acceptable is when it's warranted—i.e., someone specifically asks for it. Until then, STOP WITH THE PENIS PICTURES.

Ever jerked or sucked a guy off so hard that he blew a load past his shoulder?

It's Not Just Me: Melody, 25

I got a message from a man who liked my T-shirt, which was emblazoned with "KC" inside a heart. He'd graduated from the University of Kansas, and I'd moved to Washington DC from Kansas City, so we chitchatted about the Midwest before he casually asked if he could take me out. I said sure, then gave him my number. He seemed normal, and it's no secret that I want to settle down with a Midwestern man someday.

He texted me that afternoon and said, "Hey Melody, it's Ben." I told him I was headed to class, and he wrote, "Okay! Let me know how it goes!!!!"

I didn't let him know how it went, but he texted me anyway to ask. I said, "Oh, fine, but a three-hour class is practically a crime against humanity." To that he offered, "OR AT LEAST A CRIME AGAINST MELODY!!!!"

An hour later he sent me a picture of some flowers and said, "I took this for you!!! Be happy!!!"

I didn't respond, because by now I had that icky feeling you get when you realize you've made a huge, irritating mistake.

I ended up going out of town for a week, so the tentative date we'd planned fell through. When I was out of town, he asked, "Send me a selfie to remember you by?" (I didn't.)

When I got back I started a new job, so when he

continued to text and say, "We should hang out!!!!!" I told him I was pretty overwhelmed. Then his texts just kept asking if I was "still overwhelmed?????"

I was afraid that if I just said I wasn't interested, things would get weirder, so I blocked his number, then blocked him on OKCupid when he continued trying to reach me there. He even made an all-new account and sent me an all-new message, acting as though he'd never seen me before. This psychopath is what drove me to sign off from all online dating platforms for good. Or . . . for now.

On Basic Bros

I've taken a moment to compile a short list of characteristics that a "basic bro" (aka a male version of a "basic bitch") may possess. You're welcome!

- Daily uniform is plaid shorts and flip-flops . . . even in November

- The high point of his week is *Monday Night Football*

- Gets extremely defensive if someone has the audacity to mistakenly think he's gay

- Wouldn't be caught dead at an indie movie, a play, or any sort of cultural event that doesn't involve hot chicks or random occasional shrieks of "WOOOOOOOO!"

- Doesn't use "your"/"you're" correctly (and legit doesn't understand the difference between the two)

- Is a master of the shirtless mirror selfie

- Catcalls women (and refers to it as a "compliment" if someone busts him for it)

- Will try to talk to (er, harass?) a female even if the only thing they have in common is the fact that they're both, arguably, human

- Preferred subjects of conversation extend to favorite sports bars, the comparative glory of ales and stouts, and extolling the virtues of "ass" vs. "pussy"

- Exists entirely on a diet of meat, and thinks eating a cow is oh-so-manly

- Routinely buys kegs for parties

- Sends a first online message that goes a little something like this: "Hi ur beautiful," "Hi I'm mike. I'm new to this and have to say u caught my eye right away," "Hi, I told my mom you're my girlfriend so we need to met ASAP! Just kidding," "Hello you remind me of a better looking krysten Ritter," "Hi there the names Tom how are you today?"

THEY REALLY SAID THIS.
PART 10

Pardon me, but would you by any chance be interested in corresponding with a view to obtaining one another's numerical communication codes to our respective devices for mutual gain?

I get tons of messages from girls *and* guys asking how to construct the "perfect message" online, asking how to create the most irresistible profile, or simply seeking out general tips. Of course I have opinions on those things, because I have opinions on everything—but I think it all depends on what your intentions are. Also, what works on your profile differs between men and women, so consider that, too. There is no black-and-white answer, but if you're mainly looking to attract more interest, start with the tips below.

1. **Have good photos.** Make sure you have a variety of high-quality photos (preferably ones of you with actual teeth in your mouth. A complete set). This means more than three pictures that are not from more than a year ago, pixelated, or extremely filtered. Save the sunglasses and group shots for another day, and make sure you are giving an accurate representation of yourself. There is nothing more awkward than meeting someone in person who looks nothing like what they claimed. I don't know anyone

who would go on a first date with a someone (let alone message them back) who doesn't have clear photos on their profile.

2. BE GENUINE—and be interesting. I've actually been asked by several media outlets what tricks there are for scheming the system to rack up more messages. I was confused by the question, because I was honestly just being myself when I wrote my profile. But in any case, make sure to be concise; nobody wants to read your memoir. Stick to the point, and remember that other members have no idea who you are. Writing that you "like to travel" doesn't give a full picture of your fantastically unique personality. Tell everyone about something the next guy or girl doesn't have, something you're proud of that doesn't include your three degrees, your nice car, or the oh-so-enviable factoid that you work out seven days a week. Be humble. And be sure to avoid generic phrases like "I'm lovin' life" and "I like to laugh" because, duh, the last forty people wrote the same thing, and if you don't like to laugh, then who are you even? In my profile I wrote about the little things I enjoy, like Sour Patch Kids, down comforters, astronomy, and hockey, because it gives a real vibe of who I am.

3. Use proper grammar and spelling on your profile. Enough said. Spell-check that shit if you have to. Know the difference between "its" and "it's" (or at least Google it for your profile).

4. Send respectful messages. Whether male or female, it is not recommended that you send something along the lines of "I'd totally bang you." This shouldn't even have to be said, but apparently it does: Stay away from objectifying someone and don't rely solely on complimenting their physical appearance. Introduce yourself and say why you're interested in meeting that person, but don't write an essay. Realize that if you want to talk to

someone just because you like the way they look, you might not have enough in common.

5. If your chosen dating service has them, answer the "match-quotient" or compatibility questions. Those seemingly silly questions are there so they can match you with people who you'll potentially get along with. I also will most likely never message or respond to someone who's less than an 80 percent match with me. While I don't necessarily believe in the scientific accuracy of OKCupid's compatibility system, I do believe it is a good way to weed out people that have nothing in common with you.

6. Understand that you can't control others, only yourself. Even if you have a great profile or seem to have a stellar mental connection with someone, attraction is important, and if it's not there, it's not going to work. I've tried dating guys who I wasn't that physically into and it never seems to pan out, no matter how cool I think he is. If someone just isn't that into you, let them feel that way; don't try to force it. There have also been occasions when I was planning to respond (and just hadn't yet because I was busy) but then the guy messed shit up by deciding to jump the gun and write me again—sometimes several more times—without my response. If you send two messages and someone doesn't respond, move along and assume they're not interested.

It's important to remember that even if you're a smart, wonderful, gorgeous person and you follow all my advice, not everyone is going to fall in love with you. You can't let that affect your confidence. Everyone gets rejected, and putting your ego aside will help you in the end. You deserve someone who shows interest in truly knowing YOU.

5 Ways to Know
When It's Time to Stop
Messaging Someone

I know how hard it is out there. You're drowning in competition, people get tons of messages, and you feel like you have to be quick and funny and hot and active and skinny and, like, INSTANTLY catch someone's eye if you want to have a flying chance at keeping a conversation going. But sadly, things won't always go your way, and the assholes you write to aren't always going to respond the way you want them to. Here are a few resounding signs that it's time to put the dating app away and go do something else. (Oh, and stop messaging me, SexyBiker4u.)

❶ You've written them more than once with no response. Sorry, man. It's a no-go. Walk away.

❷ If s/he disappears in mid-conversation. Sure, you can send one follow-up message if you really, really want to, but don't expect anything. People are flaky on these sites; they pull the ghosting act constantly for a myriad of dumb reasons. Don't take it personally.

❸ The responses begin devolving from longer messages filled with normal, complete

sentences to mini-messages made up of
two- and three-word responses. S/he may be
slightly unsure about you—curious enough to
keep one toe in the water, at least—but do you
even want to date someone so half-assed?

❹ S/he won't agree to meet you. If you're
writing back and forth for awhile but s/he keeps
balking at meeting up in person, something's
up; maybe s/he's already dating someone, or
s/he's scared of meeting people from the
Internet (ugh—how 1999); or s/he's just not
that into you (sigh). Who knows? But you're
probably wasting your time.

❺ S/he says they're still embroiled in
drama with an ex, or just out of a relationship,
or newly divorced, or just getting back into the
dating scene after being off the market, or only
looking for new friends . . . AGH EXCUSES,
ENDLESS CRAPPY EXCUSES, ENDLESS.

THEY REALLY SAID THIS.
PART 11

Yesterday – 12:33 AM

Okay I'm in. You are rad.

In your profile I literally skipped to the last line and that's what I did with my self today literally. Would of been nice if you were along

Today – 4:52 AM

Would you be aroused if you were to receive tasteful and sexy artful nudes featuring me from time to time?

It's Not Just Me: Morgan, 35

ME, TEXTING AFTER ONE UNSUCCESSFUL DATE *[FYI, not serious about the astrologer thing—I was just being silly, but apparently he took it the wrong way.]*: I think you're a nice guy but my astrologer says I can only date Capricorns.

HIM: So do you listen to your astrologer or your heart?

HIM: Btw all my closest friends have been Capricorns and your not missing much. Just hard work and no play.

HIM: You don't even have the decency to pick up the phone after someone has thought well of you. I was hoping to tell you about an fabulous date I had planned. Now you have nothing, enjoy your food and drink with your other suitors.

HIM: I mean, who says that? You have a pretext, just be honest. Do you honestly believe such metaphysical fairy tails. If you do, then we are two different people.

HIM AGAIN: One more thing, you have no sense of adventure for a woman of your age. It's probably best you go find your alpha male provider. Bitch.

Date Makeup

So, let's say you've just made your very own fantastic new online dating profile. Now you have no idea whether to post the picture of you with no makeup on and your cat covering half your face, or the one of you half-drunk with full makeup and an amazing outfit.

I can help. Besides being popular on online dating sites, I'm also a professional makeup artist who spends hours of my day on photo shoots and with private clients. So I'd like to think I know what works in Internet-dating photos and what totally doesn't.

One of the most important aspects of Internet dating is presenting the most accurate representation of yourself. Elsewhere in this book I've explained how much it sucks to show up for a date and find someone who looks nothing like their pictures. You can avoid disappointing your date by posting a variety of clear, current photos—trust me, you'll get a lot more attention than you would if you just used a couple of blurry pics from five years ago. Your face is what makes you YOU, and it should be proudly revealed in all its glory.

Tons of clients have wanted me to do their makeup for them before a date, and I'd say about half wanted me to throw as much product on their face as possible, even when that wasn't actually who they were in their day-to-day. Obviously, I am not in a position to tell them, "No, I'm not going to do that," but in my opinion, the less, the better . . . for a date. Clean, glowing skin is what I'm passionate about and known for with my clients, and this is always my first priority for a good picture.

I sometimes love wearing weird stuff like red eye shadow and looking like a bit of an oddball. But I don't post any crazy makeup pics on OkCupid. (I once noticed a drop in messages received after I posted a Halloween photo of me wearing zombie makeup—I guess I scared some guys off.) And clean and simple is always my go-to first-date look.

So, without further ado, here are some simple guidelines for a makeup regimen that will work for profile photos AND the first date that results from it.

Foundation and skincare are KEY.

Even if you feel you have perfect skin, it can always look better. I've done makeup on hundreds of clients, from a seven-year-old to a ninety-year-old. There are very few people I didn't use foundation or at least a tinted moisturizer on, and the ones I didn't were obviously aliens from the planet of exceptionally perfect "how the fuck is your skin so good" skin.

So go to Sephora, do some experimenting, and find a foundation that works for you. Ask the salesperson for help if you're not sure what kind of coverage you want or what color looks right on you. And definitely don't let the word "foundation" scare you. They're not all heavy mattifying masks that will look like you have thirty pounds of crap on your face. Foundation is the one thing I will not be a cheapo on, because it is SOOO worth it.

Conceal and highlight.

Most of us are a different shade or tone under our eyes than on the rest of our face. It can be difficult finding the right match to cover dark spots, bags, and all those other fun things. I would suggest asking for some guidance from a professional at a makeup counter if you're having a difficult time finding a match.

As for highlighting, using a foundation two shades lighter, or an actual highlighting product in liquid form, on the tops of your cheekbones and down the center of your nose gives that natural glow and adds dimension to your face.

Optional: You can add a powder in translucent or in your skin tone on top of your cream products (also depending on skin type). If you have dry skin, though, either don't use powder or try a light mineral powder. If you have combo to oily skin, you can use a bit more powder to keep your flawless skin in check.

BLUSH.

Does blush have a bad reputation I don't know about? So many of my clients are scared of it. I can only assume their hesitation stems from lack of knowledge about what color to use or how to apply.

Your blush should be applied on the chubbiest parts of your cheeks (smile to find the right points). Make sure not to apply it any lower than your nose and not any higher than where your highlight is on the top of your cheekbone.

As far as the color, don't be afraid to experiment. You can go bronze, pink, coral, shimmery, matte, or cream. Just know that shimmer will accentuate texture and lines so if you have either of those, it's safer to stick with a matte color.

Defining your eyebrows can be the most important thing you do.

A little eye shadow or brow pencil can make all the difference. (I'm not talking about those stenciled-out Instagram eyebrows, ugh.) They should be YOUR eyebrows with a few spots filled in, maybe lengthened a bit, maybe darkened. Use a brow gel to keep them in place and your eyebrows are now "on fleek" (or whatever the fuck they say).

Apply eye shadow that matches your skin tone (or is a touch lighter) all over your lids.

This evens out the color and hides any veins. Follow that with a shade a tiny bit darker in your crease with a blending brush to define your eyes without looking like you have any makeup on. Be sure to blend, blend, and blend some more. Curl your lashes, then add some mascara on your top and bottom lashes to make your eyes pop.

For lips, I usually just keep it simple with Chap Stick, neutral gloss, or sheer lipstick.

. . . But a bold lip also looks amazing on a clean face. I don't care what you say—every single one of you looks good in a classic red lip. Thin lips, full lips, and uneven lips all look good in a red lip. If you say you don't look good in one, you're wrong; you're probably just intimidated by the idea and not used to seeing it on yourself.

So, now you're hot as hell and ready to post those pictures and go out on that date (or five). My last piece of advice: carry all the confidence in the world. Why be nervous about a guy who's most likely even more nervous about meeting you?

Foundation vs. Tinted Moisturizer vs. BB Cream vs. CC Cream vs. What the Fuck?

There are fifty million different types of shit to smooth on your face to make it look prettier. Some are organic, some claim to turn you into a unicorn, and some say they'll help you lose ten pounds overnight. You might be utterly baffled by it all, because you've already tried forty-nine million products, and you're frustrated, and I get it. Let's start with the differences between the main categories of shit to put on your face.

Foundation

The usual response I get when I say the word "foundation" is people leaping away from me in terror. Let's get one thing straight: not all foundation looks heavy, like you have four pounds of makeup on. There are so many different brands and so many different finishes and textures, you can find something that'll work, no matter what type of skin you have. Here are a few basic rules.

Finishes can include matte, satin, and dewy/ moisturizing. If you have extremely oily skin, using a dewy foundation is not the best idea unless you want to look like you just walked out of an underwater photo shoot at the Playboy mansion. On the same note, if your skin is super-dry you should not be using a matte finish foundation, which is designed to make your skin look flat and un-shiny. Matte finishes can look great on the right skin types, but on others they'll just accentuate imperfections.

Coverage is the next most important thing to keep in mind when selecting a foundation. Coverage ranges from light—i.e., your freckles are peeking through—to "I can't even see your pores because you've basically spackled cement on your face." Personally, I like a light-to-medium-coverage foundation because it looks most natural. Unless you're really going for cement face, stay away from any foundation that says it's heavy coverage.

Tinted Moisturizer

If you're looking for pretty sheer coverage, a tinted moisturizer can be used in place of foundation. But the main thing to remember is that it's a moisturizer. So if you have oily skin, you'll be heading right back to that "looking like you just walked out of a *Playboy* underwater photo shoot" scenario. If you have normal to dry skin, tinted moisturizer can be a good option if you just want a little something to even out the surface.

BB cream

BB creams (and CC creams; see next page) have become super-trendy in the past few years, but I'm calling bullshit right now. Beauty marketing schemes have been around forever, and just because there's a new name for something doesn't mean it's actually new. BB creams are more bullshitty than CC creams, and this is why: BB stands for "beauty balm," and that really means, well, whatever the brand's marketing team trying to sell it to you wants you to believe. A BB cream is really just a light-coverage foundation meant to even out your skin tone without covering it up.

CC cream

CC cream stands for "color-correcting cream," and good ones can be helpful products that serve a different purpose than foundation. If you've ever seen a green primer or purple lotion that claims to be a CC cream, they may actually do something for you. Green/yellow cancels out redness in your skin, while purple brightens, and orange/peach corrects dark brown spots.

If you see something that claims to be a CC cream but actually just looks like a natural, everyday skin color, it's most likely just using the trendy "CC" label to sell you a bottle of parabens (hint: those aren't good for your skin).

Nothing is black and white when it comes to beauty, and finding the right products can be harder than reading a page or two about them in a book that's not really about makeup. But hopefully I helped debunk a few mysteries about what you might want to put on your skin to make it look its glow-y best for that date you're about to go on with that guy who probably doesn't care what's on your face to begin with.

I Hate Lauren Urasek

On some first dates, I've spent more time wondering about whether my arm was in the most flattering position possible than listening to what the dude across from me was saying. And unless you have super-skinny arms (what are you, a Victoria's Secret Angel or something?), I think we've all done it (or, um, something like it). Insecurities can get the best of us when meeting someone new—or even when we're in an already established relationship. I've been known to fuck up both dates *and* relationships because of baggage stemming from the bullshit self-esteem issues I grew up with.

I wasn't the most socially accepted kid growing up. Being overweight and having really fucked-up teeth made me a constant target of bullying throughout grade school, hence the nagging insecurities. (Of course, it's only now that I realize nobody looks good at age thirteen, and if you did, I can only assume everything went downhill from there.)

I was born with a cleft lip, and though I had reconstructive surgery as an infant, that helped only with being able to breathe and eat correctly. The list of orthodontic apparatuses I was bestowed with was staggering, ranging from your average braces to a lip bumper to head gear to a palette expander. If you don't know what a palette expander is, I'm happy you didn't have to experience the trauma of wearing a device at the top of your mouth that your mom had to turn a literal key in every week.

With my teeth still not straight the summer before changing schools in seventh grade, I told my mom I wanted to get another surgery to "fix my lip." Little did I know the surgery would temporarily leave my face and lip more swollen and deformed than ever, for the next long-ass six months. A kid named David Turner took up the sweet pastime of throwing food at me in the cafeteria while incessantly calling me ugly and making me cry. Of course, he's now overweight and doing absolutely nothing with his life, unless you count dating a girl we grew up with who has really bad eyebrows and once told me nobody would ever like me. That's usually how it works out, right?

There was also that time Josh Schwartz created a Myspace group called "I hate Lauren Urasek" because I started talking to another guy in tenth grade . . . after kissing Josh all of once. The group managed to rack up a good six hundred members, all posting Microsoft-Paint-edited photos of me with penises in my mouth or the words "fat slut" scrawled in neon across my face. Kids and teenagers are obviously fucking assholes, and I'd like to think eventually we grow up and realize not to be such dicks. Unfortunately, not all people do.

I don't know if anyone ever fully gets over the negative experiences in their childhood, but I do know that I'm not still crying about things that happened in seventh grade. Gaining confidence certainly wasn't something that happened overnight, and it wasn't the result of one specific event. Nope, it was a culmination of lots of different experiences. I could have taken the insults and negativity I experienced (and continue to experience) as an excuse to put myself down and crawl into a hole. Instead of taking the negativity to heart, I chose to use it as fuel to make myself a better person.

Starting to figure out who I was and having the realization that it was okay if someone didn't like me were a powerful things. I started to see what confidence got me in different situations—whether it was a job interview or a date—and I try my best to continue that cycle every day.

Recently I went out with a thirty-two-year-old dude whose name I don't remember. He had awful bleach-blond, slicked-back hair and was wearing a button-up shirt that was way too small for his arms (he'd clearly put in a little too much bicep time at the gym). At this point in my life, I know what I want in a date, and I don't believe in dragging out anything you're just "ehh" about. We went for a drink, and about forty-five minutes in, he'd already made several racist and sexist comments. I didn't feel like arguing—it never changes those kinds of dicks' minds anyway—so I made a silent vow to leave as soon as I finished my drink.

If you've ever been on a date you're not into, you know how awkward it can be—you don't want to be an ass and bail after fifteen minutes, but you also don't want to waste your time. In the past, I would have waited it out and possibly given the guy false hope for a second date, but I've learned that my time is worth more than being bored out of my brain, and really, everyone deserves honesty. I told the super bro-y douchebag, who happened to be drinking a beer and whiskey at the same time, that I was going to leave because I had work early and I just didn't think we had that much in common, though I appreciated him coming out. He just stared at me like he had no idea what was wrong with me as I politely said 'bye and left.

Relieved to escape an unbearable situation and get home to Meemow the cat, I soon got a text from Muscle Man. "So did you really just have to work early, or did you leave for another reason?"

I knew I didn't need to respond—and I probably shouldn't have. But I told him (again) what I had said in person—we didn't have much in common—as well as what I didn't say in person: that he came off a bit sexist and racist. I wasn't expecting the reply that followed: "Well, you should let people know you're larger in person and you have a cleft lip."

My response: *Blocks number* (thanks, iOS 7).

Obviously I didn't appreciate what he'd said, but whatever—in the overall scheme, I knew it didn't matter what he thought of me. I wasn't into him, either! Plus, his nasty words said a whole hell of a lot more about him than me, and I knew he only felt the need to say that crap because he felt like shit about himself.

Before I made all these positive strides in self-confidence, there were multiple times in my last two serious relationships when my insecurities created a huge negative dent. Newsflash: Constantly calling yourself fat, disagreeing with compliments, and being crazy jealous pushes people away from you. The least attractive thing about any man or woman is a lack of liking themself, no matter how conventionally hot or un-hot they might be. And as corny as it may sound, if you respect yourself, others will respect you, too.

That gorgeous girl across from you on the subway or the delectable dude walking past you in the mall has their own issues and insecurities, no matter how perfect they look from the outside. Even your favorite celebrity is a regular, old human beneath the makeup, Photoshop, and fancy clothes—they might even be *more* insecure than you or me—with all those insane eyes on them all the time, all those fans expecting them to constantly look and act a certain way.

When you stop comparing yourself to other people, explore who you are as a person, and start being cool with the unique qualities that make you YOU, you *will* find your confidence. You'll start realizing that not being intimidated by anyone—in any situation, whether it's a bitchy new boss or those aforementioned Victoria's Secret models (I actually had to rub lotion on their cellulite-free legs once for work)—can not only help you feel infinitely more serene in your own skin, it can also help you create opportunities you never thought possible.

I'm human, so, sure, sometimes I might think I need a flatter stomach and an ass like Beyoncé, but honestly? If given the opportunity, I wouldn't take it. I love who I am these days, and I know I've gotten to this place in my life because of *me*—learning to face my own demons and conquer my own issues. In other words, I'm where I am because of the rejection I've faced, the lips I was born with, and even that gross "I hate Lauren Urasek" Myspace group.

THEY REALLY SAID THIS.
PART 12

Jan 17 7:33 PM
Hey gorgeous

Jan 29 7:59 AM
Hey gorgeous

Feb 02 2:32 PM
Howdy gorgeous

Feb 10 6:16 PM
Hey gorgeous

Dudespeak

Some guys on dating sites tend to speak in code. This code might seem inscrutable at first, but spend enough time sifting through crap messages from irritating (and transparent) people, and you'll start to figure out what they're truly trying to say. Here are a few notable lines from messages I've received or profiles I've come across, and a helpful translation of what they're really saying.

I want to meet you if you're really just up for meeting new people, seeing what all is out there in this great world.

TRANSLATION: I just got out of a long-term relationship and my heart's currently smashed into miniscule, papery bits. I'd love to use this dating app to find some new distractions to stick my penis in until I've realized I'm not ready for even a hint of companionship or commitment.

My ideal woman is active and takes care of herself.
TRANSLATION: My ideal woman must be a slave to fitness and, more importantly, skinny as shit. No fatties, please, and if you have cellulite on your ass, it's a definite NO.

Hi there , how are you ? [Sent Aug 14]
Hi there , how are you ? [Sent Oct 31]
TRANSLATION: My brain is mush.

I'm living my life to the fullest!!

TRANSLATION: I'm an overgrown man-child who drinks until 6:00 AM and then passes out surrounded by my four roommates. Occasionally I go on a vacation to Miami and think it's exotic.

What a snarky profile, I liked it!

TRANSLATION: I'm not used to confident women who have strong opinions, but I'm finding it hot, even though in person I would be extremely insecure around you.

I'm a pretty spontaneous guy who is ALL ABOUT excitement . . . and adventure.

TRANSLATION: I'm an ADHD-addled Peter Pan who will unabashedly check out other women on our first date.

Do you want to be part of a fantasy I have? It's a really good deal for you.

TRANSLATION: I have an obsession with performing oral sex on women.

Message me if you're interested in hooking up. Long term sex-based relationship with good conversation preferred.

TRANSLATION: I actually want a girlfriend, but the second you call yourself that I'm running really far away.

Nice tats.

TRANSLATION: I've always wanted to have sex with a girl who has tattoos.

You're adorable! So adorable I want to adopt you as my little sister. Don't worry we'll spend all our time climbing trees and drinking Kool-Aid. But seriously, you seem like a cool person. I'd love to get together and let you cook for me haha . . . WAIT! You're not crazy are you?

TRANSLATION: I'm a sexist pedophile.

Looking forward to meeting you if . . . you know how to loosen up and have a good time.

TRANSLATION: I think any female that wants any sort of commitment is an uptight bitch.

That Time I Got Dumped Because "It Just Wasn't Right"

I met Ethan on OKCupid, and I'd rate our first date a decidedly "meh" five out of ten stars. I decided to give him a second chance, though, regardless of the fact that I wasn't really looking for anything serious. He was good-looking, smart, and attentive, and I had nothing to lose. I hate that corny cliché: You "find someone when you least expect it!!!," but, well, in this scenario, that's kind of what happened.

On our second date, Ethan took me to a great little sushi place in the Lower East Side. He did all the right things—he complimented me, insisted we order dessert, and took me to a cool speakeasy after dinner—but he wasn't fully opening up, and I was on the fence about the chemistry factor. Still, I was used to having to take control on most of my dates (steer the conversation, decide where we went and when we'd meet), so being with someone a little more take-charge was a nice change. Plus, Ethan dressed well, lived alone (a huge deal for young, New York guys), and seemed like he knew what he wanted. As most women will concur, confidence can boost a dude's overall appeal from a seven to a solid ten.

After dinner, we sat at the bar drinking bourbon as he rambled about—of all things—his stripper ex-girlfriend. Ew, really? *Please don't ruin this,* I thought. Everyone knows—or *should* know—not to bring up exes until later (if ever).

"She was a cool girl, but she was only twenty-three, so obviously she was pretty immature," he explained about why they'd broken up two months earlier. I was almost the same age as his ex, so I got pretty irritated by his inference that all women our age were too childish to have our shit together.

Was this the first sign that Ethan wasn't ready for a Real Thing? Or just a sign that he liked much younger girls? Which honestly can be a bit creepy in its own right. Whatever it was, he was eleven years older than me, and apparently most of his friends were also single. In other words, he perfectly met the criteria of that stereotypical bachelor guy in his mid-to-late thirties who "never wants to settle down."

Normally, all those red flags would have sent me begging for the check within thirty minutes, but somehow Ethan charmed me into staying longer, and that first drink turned into a second drink, then a third.

We moved from the bar to one of the super-comfy red velvet couches in the back, where we eventually strayed from the loaded ex-girlfriend subject and moved into more neutral topics like our mutual interest in *Breaking Bad*, spending time outdoors, and the boundless virtues of thin-crust pizza. Maybe it was all the bourbon, or maybe I was genuinely curious to know more, but I ended up walking back to Ethan's Lower East Side apartment with him that night. I almost felt like I was in high school again—I stayed over, and our first kiss was in his very bachelor-like bed, but that's as far as it went.

The next morning felt remarkably . . . un-awkward. I didn't have that usual morning-after urgency to flee, which is a pretty big deal, to be honest. I started to rethink my stance on this guy even more.

We walked to a little French luncheonette for breakfast in SoHo, and Ethan even fucking held an umbrella for me as we walked in the early-summer rain. It all seemed too good to be true, but the idea of having a guy to roam around New York City with during the hot, sticky season was admittedly pretty enchanting, and we started hanging out several times a week. I slowly became addicted to the feeling of having, yes, a significant other (ugh).

I remember looking into Ethan's eyes one night about three weeks after we'd started dating. We were standing on a street corner in the East Village waiting to cross the street, when I suddenly thought, *I love this guy*. I didn't say it out loud—only crazies or self-sabotagers say that shit mere weeks into a relationship—but I was surprised by how strongly I felt it.

Weeks turned into months, and Ethan made me so happy, I was walking around with a huge perma-smile, because I couldn't believe everything was going so . . . right. There was just one thing that bothered me.

One night when he was introducing me to some of his friends, he announced, "This is my friend Lauren." I gave him a look, like, "Really? Your fucking *friend*?" We'd been seeing each other for at least two months by then—and almost every fucking day, no less.

I confronted him the next morning. Was he *that* afraid of commitment that he couldn't bear to call me his girlfriend? "To call someone my friend is actually a big deal to me, and you should be fine with that," he kept pleading, and there wasn't any satisfying resolution to the conversation. I was frustrated, but still not ready to let go, and he didn't seem up for walking away, either. Maybe he needed a little longer to get over his ex, or maybe he needed more time for the proverbial lightbulb to go off about how great of a girlfriend I was. (Pro tip: "More time" is never enough.)

A couple weeks later I was planning a trip to Vegas for my birthday with my best friend Kathleen. Ethan took me out for a great dinner and got me an awesome present, too: a pretty blue butterfly in a shadow box. I'd briefly mentioned how much I liked them when we first started dating, and he'd actually remembered. But still, I was so confused about "what we were" that I felt like maybe I should just start acting like Single Lauren again. Er, at least while I was on vacation?

There's nothing worse than being vulnerable and giving all of yourself to someone when they refuse to give it back to you. So I took a little bit of space; if he wasn't committing to me fully, I wasn't going to, either.

On my actual birthday in Vegas, Kathleen and I decided to be spontaneous and do something we wouldn't normally do. I'm not a club-goer by any stretch, but somehow it seemed appropriate in Vegas. As we were waiting to get in, I jokingly noted, "All I want for my birthday is a hot, tattooed Australian." Kathleen replied with a laugh, "Good luck with that."

The club was packed with muscle-y, tribal-tattooed guidos and girls in white shorts and chunky glitter heels. Luckily, we had some free-drink tickets, because otherwise the watered-down liquor was going for twenty dollars a glass. We needed some dudes to buy us drinks, stat.

Less than fifteen minutes later, I turned around and saw a very attractive, heavily tattooed dude staring at me. "Hey," the super-tall, super-well-dressed guy blurted out in—you guessed it—an Australian accent. Either the universe was on my side, or a lot of hot Australians visit Vegas in July. Or both?

The night wound up being pretty insane. The Australian gave me four hundred dollars to gamble with, which I lost at the blackjack table within ten minutes. (Dudes, take note: It's not in your best interests to give gambling money to random drunk girls in Vegas, even if you think they might sleep with you.) Even though it was 4:00 AM, he was wearing sunglasses on the top of his head. I gave him shit for that, then confessed that I actually liked them. "Happy birthday—they're yours," he proclaimed as he handed them to me. Any lingering thoughts of Ethan were gone by then. Rather drunk, I followed the Australian back to his room, because what better way to end an amazing night than with a ton of hot hotel sex overlooking a floor-to-ceiling view of the sunrise over the Nevada mountains?

I knew Ethan would probably feel pretty shitty if he knew what I'd done, but I wasn't his girlfriend and I didn't think I owed him anything. If I'd had complete confidence in us, I wouldn't have even talked to the Australian, but Ethan wasn't going to have his cake and eat it, too. I know some people might consider this "cheating," but I think it's perfectly acceptable to do what you want until you've discussed with your partner that you're mutually exclusive.

Back home in New York, Ethan and I kept seeing each other, and I tried to stop worrying about the whole girlfriend/ boyfriend thing. I was actually *happy* with a guy for once—he treated me so well, taking me out to dinner at night and brunch on the weekends. We spent days upon days together contentedly doing nothing, and we supported each other when one of us felt shitty about work, family, or whatever.

Finally, after about four months of knowing Ethan, he described me as his girlfriend to an acquaintance. I was jumping up and down on the inside, and I assumed that everything would naturally be even more amazing from then on out. And things *did* stay amazing, for at least a couple more months.

We planned a vacation, I met his family on Thanksgiving, and we exchanged those three terrifying little words: "I love you." However scary they seemed, I was 100 percent sure about it.

About a week before Christmas, Kathleen had a Christmas party. Ethan seemed off the whole night, but he wouldn't tell me what was up, so I guessed he must just be stressing about work, which wasn't uncommon. The next afternoon, I sent him a text asking if he wanted to relax and watch a movie that night. He responded with a terse "OK," which was . . . not like him. He'd usually add a bit more to the conversation or send me a link to some cool article, so a one-word response was weird.

When I arrived at his apartment that night, before I could even take off my coat, he started mumbling in a trembling voice. "It's not working—something just doesn't feel right," he admitted as he took sip after sip from a glass of water. He was sitting on his couch and wouldn't make eye contact with me.

"What are you talking about?" I repeated over and over. I

was completely baffled—and heartbroken. We never fought, and nothing like this had ever come out of his mouth before. All he kept saying was that I was the best girlfriend he'd ever had, that I did so much for him. "Then why are you doing this?" I asked.

I cried in his arms. He cried, too, telling me he didn't want to end it, but it was for my own good. The only justification he gave was that he knew I was putting more into the relationship; it wasn't fair to me, and I deserved someone who would treat me better than he did. I couldn't wrap my mind around that, because I'd never been treated as well as Ethan had treated me.

I took a cab home, crying the entire way, and I must have stayed in my bed for a week with swollen eyes and dirty clothes. All my friends were just as confused, and even Stephanie, one of Ethan's friends whom I'd become close with, texted to let me know that it was just as much a surprise for her.

Even though we had dated for about six months, it took the same amount of time to get over him. And though it was a pretty short-lived relationship by most standards, it affected me more than any other breakup ever had. I only realized what had actually gone wrong after I'd had months to mull it over.

Even though I was happy with Ethan, I'd been miserable at work and not taking care of myself—I'd been eating like shit and feeling awful about my body. So I ended up focusing all my energy on Ethan, which ultimately grew unhealthy. He had so many things going on—a great job, awesome friends—and all I had going for me was . . . him. At least that's what I thought at the time. I didn't realize that being in a successful relationship means having your shit together first—you shouldn't be looking for a partner to complete you, but to complement you.

Plus, aside from my four-year-long thing with Christian, I'd had no other real relationship to compare Ethan to. He wasn't a pathologically lying drug addict, which, sadly took him a long way with me. Maybe the only reason I fell so deeply in love with Ethan was because he actually treated me with a modicum of respect. I can't say for sure why I felt the way I did, but I do know I'll never prioritize a guy over my own well-being again.

how many expensive sushi dinners would it take to for you to be my own bedroom acrobat for many years to come?

Millions.

Cupcakes and Whores

The night of my big birthday party was finally here.

Of course I'd built up great expectations for the night—expectations that probably wouldn't be met—but I was excited nonetheless. One of my favorite things in life is planning a good party, and despite my lack of budget, I thought I'd done an OK job. It was a perfect end-of-summer night, I'd managed to book a cool outdoor space in Manhattan, and I was wearing an impeccably planned and executed outfit. What more could I have asked for?

After being unceremoniously ousted by Ethan, I'd been single for a while by then, and I had finally come to accept it. There's something about feeling confident on your birthday and hanging out with a bunch of great friends that makes being unattached feel pretty fun. In lieu of a boyfriend, I would opt for tequila and cupcakes, knowing full well that neither of them would ultimately disappoint me.

My friend Rachel, whom I had seen maybe three times in the past five years, came up to visit from Maryland for the weekend. She was the ballsy, beautiful, rebellious blond chick who had always stood up for me when kids were assholes growing up. For the longest time, if you Googled "Lauren Urasek," a Xanga post would pop up from Rachel's blog saying, "Whoever is fucking with Lauren Urasek at school needs to die." (Xanga, if you don't recall, was the baby predecessor of Myspace. You couldn't even post pictures on it, and every thirteen-year-old in the country would write lengthy, painfully boring updates about their unbearably boring days.)

My relationship with Rachel spanned back to middle school, when I'd gotten drunk with her for the first time off of a forty-ounce Smirnoff Ice in a 7-Eleven parking lot. Nowadays I actually attribute my fine ability to handle liquor to all the beatings we put our bodies through when we were fourteen. I was pretty much over the thrill of drinking by the time I was seventeen, which probably helped me get my shit together before some of my peers. Between skipping school for no good reason to taking shots of Everclear on the boardwalk, Rachel and I had quite the colorful history.

We got ready at my apartment with a bottle of wine and reminisced about our youthful obnoxiousness. "When I have kids, I'm putting them on lockdown in my house and never letting them out," Rachel said.

I agreed: "We got lucky for not turning into teen moms or complete fuckups." Even though it might sound like I was a horrible kid, I'd done pretty well in school, getting As and Bs and participating in TAG (Talented and Gifted) classes. Whoever the fuck came up with "TAG" sure knew how to make all the other kids feel like shit.

Rachel started telling me about a dude, Anthony, she'd just started talking to. They had met only once but were texting constantly. "He is *so* different, Lauren. I've never met a guy who was so nice and respectful."

"Ah, that's nice." My curt answer was a result of my cynical perspective on these types of scenarios. You know, the whole "guy you've been texting for days or even weeks on end that seems totally perfect at first, but ends up to be entirely the opposite of that"? I've had my fair share of dudes I immediately connected with online—ones who cured my loneliness for a good week before they magically transformed into something else during our first meet-up.

Every time Rachel mentioned how great this guy was, my own shitty experiences played in my head, making me feel a twinge of guilt. Maybe I was being too negative? After all, neither of them lived in New York City, so ostensibly they weren't completely cursed in the romantic department. Rachel mentioned that her new dude was on vacation just north of NYC and wanted to stop by to see her that weekend.

I remember only the first hour of my party, which tells you most of what you need to know about the evening. I saw a ton of friends and acquaintances who bought me shot after shot. Flash forward to 3:00 AM, when my friend Nicky's friend invited us to a bar that was open after-hours (the legal closing time for NYC bars is 4:00 AM). Though on most nights I'm actually home by ten, it was my birthday, and why the fuck would I *not* be out ruining my liver all night (and into the morning)? This city really doesn't sleep—not because of the horrid twenty-four-hour lights in Times Square, but because of the vast amount of drugs people do, and the fact that you're able to order a platter of sushi at any hour, day or night.

Once Rachel, Nicky, and I arrived at the venue, I realized it wasn't a bar but an apartment. I first noticed the makeshift walls, which were half-assedly painted a dirty shade of brown, and who could forget those nasty tile floors from 1982. The guys who invited us there were exactly who you'd expect when you hear the phrase "large, manly, and tattooed."

About ten of us hung out in the living room, and while it wasn't a party by any means, being at some unknown apartment that I felt like I didn't belong in brought me back to all those random high school parties with Rachel. I asked the group, "So, whose place is this?"

"It's just a space we hang out at," one of the dudes said.

So you all pay thousands of dollars to rent an apartment you "hang out at"? I thought, confused. Most people in New York can barely afford their rent, let alone maintain some janky secondary space in midtown for no real reason.

An older woman entered the room with a rolling cart full of every type of alcohol you could imagine. She was in her fifties with giant bags under her eyes that made it look like she hadn't slept in weeks, and she was wearing an old T-shirt and wrinkled baby-blue velour sweatpants. I declined the alcohol she offered because, well, I was already drunk. Not sure what to think, I took a trip to the bathroom, heading down a long hallway that seemed like it was under renovation.

Making my way back down the creepy hallway to the living room, I saw a chick who could only be described as "classy as fuck." And by "classy" I mean she had no pants on, had long, greasy hair, was wearing a tattered T-shirt, and clearly couldn't care less that I could basically see her vagina.

I was obviously overdressed for whatever was happening in this sketchy scenario, and I was OK with that. One of the guys there stopped me. "Hey," he nodded his head downward at a sandwich bag he was holding that was full of white powder. It was obvious anyone with that much cocaine was dealing it, and I started laughing, suddenly realizing the old woman was a madam, the half-naked chick was a prostitute, and that I had unknowingly ended up in an actual whorehouse on my twenty-fourth birthday.

I finally found Nicky and Rachel, who kept repeatedly exclaiming, "Where the fuck are we?!" We were laughing too hard to realize we should probably just leave, but I didn't feel in danger or anything. Nicky's guy friends were actually treating us like queens, constantly asking if we wanted anything, and the madam and the Pantsless Wonder stayed in the back of the apartment. It may not have been as organized as the Bunny Ranch but it definitely wasn't as bad as some of the shit I've seen on the National Geographic Channel. After another half hour or so, we decided to head home.

Rachel and I got back to my apartment at sunrise, only to wake up around noon still drunk. Naturally, we ordered pizza and mozzarella sticks.

"So, Anthony's bus will be here in a few hours."

"Who's Anthony?"

"The guy I've been telling you about all weekend? You said it was cool if he stayed with us tonight. He can leave with me tomorrow."

Blurred memories of the night before came rushing back. Rachel had been texting him during my party and had asked me if it was okay if he stayed at my place that night. I'd actually gotten on speakerphone with him and told him he could come hang out as long as he didn't "fucking suck," and if he did suck, I would kick him out and make him get a hotel. You can call me the gentle-and-understanding type, obviously.

I don't even like family and friends staying at my apartment, though, let alone strangers; when someone is sleeping on my couch, not only can I not walk around my apartment in my underwear, but I feel the need to be constantly accommodating and responsible for their comfort. I immediately regretted telling Anthony he could stay. I mean, I didn't know who this dude was, and the previous night had produced a hangover that would last for at least forty-eight hours.

Rachel and I headed out to brunch with a few other friends, but almost as soon as we got there, she had to leave to pick up Anthony from the bus station. Most people visiting NYC underestimate the inconvenience of going back and forth from Manhattan to Brooklyn. Especially with a slew of luggage—it's actually the definition of hell. I warned her, but she insisted she'd pick him up, go back to my apartment to drop off his shit, then come back out to Manhattan to meet up with us.

Several hours later, they showed up to meet Kathleen and me. My first impression of Anthony was, well, "ugh." He looked like he hadn't showered in days, and his Aéropostale sleeveless T-shirt exaggerated his deodorant-encrusted armpit hair. He was hanging all over Rachel in the creepiest way possible, acting like they'd been together for years. He kept trying to kiss her and look deeply into her eyes every two seconds. You may think that sounds sweet, but trust me, you too would have been compelled to make a face like you'd just seen a homeless man shit on the street.

He kept talking about wanting to get drunk and nagging me to find someone in the city to buy drugs from. Rachel knew I was annoyed, but I couldn't tell how she felt about the situation. Of course, though I'd said the night before that I would kick him out if he sucked, I'm not going to leave someone out on the street in an unfamiliar city just because their personality is shitty, so I begrudgingly let him come home with us, where he slept on the couch, continued nagging me about drugs, kept hanging all over Rachel, and then snored for the entire four hours or so that we managed to sleep.

Rachel later told me they didn't wind up working out (*Obviously*, I thought. She was far too good for him). It only reaffirmed my hard-won cynicism that having these one-to-two-week romances via text does not usually translate into a successful real-life relationship.

I woke up the next morning to the sight of a repulsive, shirtless man standing over my bed bugging me about how to work my coffee maker, and I silently vowed that this would Never. Happen. Again.

I absolutely love the tats

Wouldn't mine ripping your clothes off of you

I really need an amazing blowjob today . . . can you help me out

No. I can't help you out.

He's Only in It for the Sex If . . .

❶ He follows a shit-ton of random girls he's never met on Instagram. Many of said girls have a penchant for excessive use of exclamation points, kissy-face emojis, and hashtags like #followme, #fit, #werkit, and #hottie.

❷ His text messages consist of three words or less, and they magically arrive primarily between the golden hours of midnight and four in the morning.

❸ When you're staying over at his place, he's in a rush to get you out because he "has to be at work crazy early" or "has soooooooooo much to do" that day.

❹ He won't ever pay for anything. Not your coffee, or margarita, the tip, or . . . yeah, anything.

❺ He only talks about himself and never asks you a question. Not even ONE. MEASLY. QUESTION.

❻ He's less than interested when you're bothered by something.

The Supremely Awkward
Three-Date Breakup

We've all been dumped, including me. (And of course I've done my fair share of the dumping, too—who hasn't?) To me, the most breathtakingly awkward breakup scenario is when you're trying to extricate yourself from something with someone you've only gone on a handful of less-than-remarkable dates with. Maybe you're into it and he's feeling meh, or he's feeling it and you're still figuring it out, or maybe you're both doing that uncomfortably ambivalent thing. There are generally a few (mega-awkward) ways this variety of short-term, confrontation-avoiding romantic ousting can go. Take note.

The Vanishing

You've gone out with a guy a few times, but you can't fully tell if he's liking what you're selling. You have a great time when you see him, he seems into you, he pays for dinner, and you've even made out a couple of times. But when you're not together, he suddenly becomes flaky and hard to pin down. Then, without warning, poof! He's gone. No more texts, no more messages, and certainly no calls (are there ever calls?). You think about texting him to ask what's up, but instead you decide to just say fuck it and let him be. It's frustrating and annoying that he didn't even have the nerve to give you an explanation, but you know that you are, of course, better off without the bullshit.

The Put-Off

Say you're seeing someone you're still not sure about. You keep thinking you'll give it one more good, old college try. *Maybe just oooooone more date and the magic attraction fairy will make it wondrously materialize!* you keep reassuring yourself. Because HE'S SUCH A GOOD GUY. The kind of guy you SHOULD, like, SHOULD be with. But nope, after a few go-rounds it's clear that the love just isn't there. Still, you don't have the heart to tell that to the poor sap. He's SO GODDAMN NICE, remember? He doesn't deserve the pain. So instead of letting him down gently or just pulling a Vanish, you keep making excuses to avoid him. It's like the old "washing my hair" crap from the '50s or whenever—it sucks and it makes you look like a capricious tool, so don't do it.

The Painful Honesty

The final—and arguably kindest—way to get rid of someone is to do the unthinkable: Simply tell them the truth. Well, some variation of the truth, at least. Please *don't* mention it if he has a large mole on his chin that you can't stop staring at excessively, or if you just don't appreciate the odor streaming from his enlarged pores.

Conclusion

Next time you get a nice-ish message from your latest three-date wonder confessing something like, "You're an awesome lady, but I just don't think I'm feeling that proverbial spark," thank him for his candor and be on your way (even if that's just to bed or another *Breaking Bad* binge). It always sucks less to KNOW one way or the other.

have you ever been with an sexually dominant guy who is extremely abusive in the bedroom

Do you want to murder me?

It's Not Just Me: Buffy, 35

I'm not proud of this story, but I'd just broken up with my fiancé, and I was a little angry at men. I went out on a date with this guy I met online who was really hot, but I knew he was a bartender and probably really sleazy—I didn't care because I didn't plan to sleep with him.

The guy got wasted and started talking about being in the army, making references to militias and stuff. At one point he mentioned "the brotherhood." Then he randomly pulled up his shirt and he had a swastika tattoo. I'm half Jewish from my dad's side, and obviously I was horrified—I'd never met anyone who goes around talking openly about being a Nazi. I should have walked out, but I didn't. I guess I wanted to see what else he'd say, how far he would take it, and whether he was even serious. So I played along and said, "Tell me more."

He said that he and his brother were in the Aryan Brotherhood, and that they had killed black people. He talked a lot about jail. I thought he was fucking with me, because honestly, what he was saying was so outrageous I could hardly believe any of it. It wasn't like we were living in Mississippi; we were in DC, for god's sake. The more he talked, the more disgusted I felt, but I still played along, because I was so curious by then; I felt like I couldn't stop the crazy train.

I asked him if he'd take me to one of his Aryan meetings, and he was like, "I can't just take *anyone* there."

I replied, "Dude, look at me. Blond hair, blue eyes. I'm your sister in this battle."

I guess I was convincing, because he agreed to introduce me to some of his Aryan freak friends sometime. We were in his car by then, and he kept trying to make out. He actually pulled out his dick within, like, two minutes—I guess by then he thought I was "the one" or something. I leaned down like I was actually considering putting it in my mouth, then stopped abruptly and said, "So you wanna get your dick sucked by a Jew?"

He laughed and said, "Stop fucking with me."

I was like, "Um, I'm not fucking with you."

His face went red. I got out of the car and started busting ass to get out of there. I heard his car screech— he made a U-turn and yelled at me to get the fuck back in the car. I ran into a restaurant and he finally left, but later that night he actually sent me a text saying to let him know if I wanted to hook up again sometime.

On Trusting Your Gut

I f there's one thing going out with a bountiful and sometimes terrifying medley of New York City dudes has taught me, it's the importance of trusting your gut and not wasting valuable time on vapid, meaningless relationships.

Unfortunately, it's a lesson I've mainly learned in hindsight. For some reason, it's incredibly difficult advice to follow in the moment, no matter how crucial you know it is. Trust me, though. Your gut usually knows best, and all those cues—both verbal and nonverbal—that your date is sending you are worth heeding before you pass judgment about whether you'll go out with them in the first place or continue dating.

1) Note any subtle (or not-so-subtle) text warnings before you meet in person.

It happens all too often: I find someone online who I think could be great. In his profile the guy seems smart, alluring, and genuine (added bonus points when we have a match percentage of, like, 90+, which *really* doesn't happen often). So I send a quick, thoughtful message to get the conversation rolling. If he seems normal, we'll move on to exchanging phone numbers, then we'll text. That's when I tend to determine that yes, I'd like to meet up with this person or no, they've said something asinine that completely messed with my interest in meeting them. (At that point, even if some tiny part of me is still on the fence about whether I should give him a chance, I heed my internal warning signs. Because red flags are there for a reason.) A few select lines that have made me flip on wanting to meet a dude in person:

> "I'm not too proud to admit when I'm wrong. It's just never happened."

> "I'm sorry, but I will not be able to meet you for that drink. I can't do that to my girlfriend."

> "Would you like to adventure around the city with me and get into some TROUBLE?!!"

> "I believe in God."

> "U should ask why I'm so cute."

> "I'm very physically busy all day so I kind of neglect my phone most of the day."

> "Hung like a donkey."

2) And the verbal warnings when you do meet face-to-face.

When I showed up to meet Dan at a local coffee shop, I was surprised to find an adorable, stylish, strong-jawed dude in a worn-down baseball hat. Sure, he'd looked cute enough in his pictures, but I wasn't expecting him to be *this attractive* (for some reason I'd been worried his neck would be really long).

The conversation flowed easily, and I was put at ease when I realized he was as smart as his profile had made him sound. But quickly enough, little flags began springing up. For one thing, he kept name-dropping and talking about all the cool places he frequented multiple times a week. (He wasn't a fan of staying home and chilling—apparently ever.) But . . . shouldn't you be past your "getting wasted every night phase"? I'm only twenty-four, and I'm already rapidly moving beyond that shit. He also mentioned talking to women at bars a lot. Not picking them up, per se, but chatting them up, which to me read as essentially the same thing. If we're on a date, I don't need to hear about it, buddy.

It started to become evident that he wasn't open to an actual relationship; instead he was poised to enter that massively unappealing "I'm in my late thirties, still have roommates, and act like I'm twenty-two" stage, just like so many other guys in big cities.

3) Listen to their body language.

Another thing it's important to pay attention to on dates is nonverbal cues. Again, that's something your gut can detect faster than your conscious, rational mind can. (When you like a guy, your conscious, rational mind is busy scrambling for validating hints that he likes you back.) Ever have a perfectly great time with a guy—good conversation, what seems like a strong connection—but for some reason you leave the date with nary the slightest of inklings about where you fucking stand or how he felt about you? That's your gut informing you it's a no-go, and it probably picked up on that, at least partially, from what the guy was saying—or not saying with words.

Not looking you in the eye, not smiling much, glancing around the room a lot, not offering to pay, not holding the door, checking his phone, declining to offer you a piece of gum when he takes one out for himself—these are all relatively negligible things that some people might say don't necessarily mean any-thing, but . . . those people are lying. If he's not making a basic effort to do things for you—to impress you, please you, win you over—on your first date, he just isn't that into you. Sorry.

4) If you "just have a feeling," follow it.

You don't owe anyone anything, and if you aren't sure about someone you barely know, don't spend your priceless energy trying to make it feel right. Perhaps not giving people enough of a chance is why I'm still single, but I've had too many boring-ass dates to get up off my couch for someone I'm ambivalent about. I used to go on tons of dates with an open mind (so innocent! so naive!) but after so many shitty ones, I decided I'd rather stay home and watch the Discovery Channel.

I'm like a snow storm, I'll give you
6 to 8 inches and keep you inside for the
whole weekend.

I hate snow storms.

Tom Hanks and Expensive Linens

Dating sites aren't the only ways people meet online. I've also been approached on Facebook, Twitter, Instagram, and even LinkedIn. (But seriously, guys in your forties who are actually married, can you *stop* harassing me on LinkedIn?)

One day I opened my often-ignored direct-message folder on Instagram to find a message from a prominent comedian—let's call him Bill (nope, that's not his real name). His note was short and, well, not especially sweet, but it was direct, which I appreciate: "Hey. We should hang out." Clearly, he'd put a lot of thought into the message, but even though I knew he was judging me superficially—in another word, solely—on my Instagram photos—I didn't really care.

I'd seen his stand-up and had actually met him once, about six months earlier, at the Comedy Cellar in New York. He was good at what he did—you could even call me a fan—but at that point I had met enough overpaid reality stars and A- to D-list celebrities that the "star factor" didn't really faze me.

I messaged him back: "Yeah, we should." For the next couple months we texted here and there, but because of our schedules, finding a time to actually meet proved tricky.

We finally pinned down a time and decided on a modern Italian restaurant for dinner and drinks. When we met in person, it felt like I'd known him for a while, which kind of made sense, since I *had* been familiar with his TV personality and stand-up. This was a new scenario for me. Typically when I meet someone for a first date I'm totally clueless about who they are, aside from what they put out there on social media, but they often know at least a little bit about me because of the whole Most-Popular-Girl-on-OKCupid situation. With Bill, I enjoyed being on the other side of the fence, and I figured maybe he would understand some of the weird shit I'd been through (like being so Google-able). Also, he was the more "popular" one at our table, and I liked that.

Bill had several stand-up shows to perform that night, so when we left the restaurant I started to head toward the train. "My first show is actually right around the corner. Want to grab a drink at the bar before I go on?" He asked. I agreed, but once we got there, I was obviously curious to see his set, so I ended up awkwardly loitering in the back of the room to catch the whole thing. Watching him do stand-up and make a huge crowd laugh at every other word out of his mouth instantly made him 5,000 percent more appealing.

After finishing his set about fifteen minutes later, he asked if I wanted to come to the next show with him. I was having so much fun doing something out of the ordinary on a Tuesday night that I enthusiastically agreed. (Why do the most interesting things always happen on Tuesdays?)

Bill and I spent the next six hours cab-hopping from show to show, from Brooklyn to Manhattan and back. He'd put his arm around me and introduced me warmly to whoever was backstage. I couldn't help but wonder if he did this with a new chick every week.

I listened to him tell the same jokes over and over again to different crowds, but somehow it didn't get old. At every venue we grabbed another drink, and at every venue we got more comfortable around each other. And by comfortable, I mean we made out in a cab and he may or may not have groped me a couple of times. But, ya know . . . whatever. I didn't know how much genuine chemistry we had, but I did know he most likely had a large penis because he was over six feet tall. I also knew that I hadn't had sex in six months, so there was that.

We were walking out of his last show when he hopped into a taxi and assumed I was getting in with him. When I said I wasn't, because: 1. It was our first date, and 2. I had to work early in the morning, he looked disappointed. He tried to convince me to change my mind. It's almost as if guys learned their BS "come over to my place and check out my Criterion Collection or my six thousand records or my extensive selection of imported vermouth" persuasion techniques from the top salesperson at a used-car dealership. I wanted to see him again, but as we all know, making it past date one is the hardest part of dating, especially in New York City.

Several days went by and Bill sent me some funny Internet video clip, but that was the extent of our contact. I don't really buy into those lame "hard to get" gender-specific dating rules, so I sent him a text: "Am I actually going to see you again, or do you just like to make out in cabs?" I decided a second date could help determine if he was looking for an actual relationship or just hoping to hang out in a vagina every once in a while. His very specific and helpful answer was, "I hope so."

"Uh, what kind of answer is that?" I wrote back, because honestly, if a dude "hopes" to see you again, he'll do the unthinkable and ask you out. He didn't respond, but two days later he texted me at nine that night saying, "Movie night!" Everyone knows that a "movie night" invite from a guy you barely know really means "I just want to fuck you," so I ignored it. Two weeks later, he again asked if I wanted to come over and watch a movie. I still wasn't interested, and I told him so. A few weeks later (apparently he was a *really* busy man) he invited me to a hockey game. Finally we weren't stuck on the movie crap! I wasn't sure what would come of this—maybe he did just want me for sex, or maybe he was just horrible at dating—but I'm always down for an NHL game.

The next day he told me he had to make an appearance at some party at the Gramercy Park Hotel before the game and invited me to join him. After I'd been waiting for fifteen minutes in one of the lobby's oversized leather chairs, watching wealthy European tourists in weird sneakers walk in and out and back again, Bill finally showed up, looking apologetic. "I'm sorry, traffic fucking sucks," he apologized, and it's worth noting that he actually seemed sincere.

I asked what the party was for, and he said it was a release party for a new phone. (Apparently, people have release parties for phones! Never would have known.) We took the elevator up to the roof deck where blue and purple lights lined temporary walls that had been constructed to block out the twenty-degree weather. There were entirely too many people crammed into the small space, and just when I thought shit might start sucking, I was relieved to see a huge table lined with champagne and any type of sushi I could possibly imagine to fulfill my deepest, darkest, carb-iest desires.

During the party, Bill introduced me to everyone, which made me feel semi-special—I'd dated guys for months who hadn't even bothered to introduce me to their closest friends. We were there for only fifteen minutes when we decided it was too packed, so we headed off to the Rangers game. When we were leaving the party, the door hostess handed us two gift bags. They each contained a fancy new cell phone with a pair of flashy, expensive headphones. I didn't really *need* a new phone (why would I give up my iPhone?), but, uh, I guess I'd take it? Apparently these were the types of arbitrary perks celebrities were showered with all the time.

When we got to the game, we were ushered through Madison Square Garden's VIP entrance, which felt, well, sur-real. The woman at the door greeted Bill like he'd been there every other day, and we ascended the elevators to be met by another attendant who escorted us to our seats. We were only four rows back from the ice. As we approached our seats, it felt like everyone in the surrounding sections was overtly staring at Bill with admiration, and some shouted out that they were "huge fans." As I walked past the people in our row, I realized that a bunch of Bill's friends were seated near us, and they were all people I'd seen on TV. Again, surreal.

On the Jumbotron they were calling out celebrities in the

audience, like they always do at sporting events. Whoa—there was Tom Hanks, grinning into a camera about twenty feet to my right. When intermission came, we were swooped away to another VIP room to hang out in. It was filled with any type of food you could want: crab claws, cheesecake, meatballs, sushi, cookies, and, of course, a fully stocked open bar. I downed my drink faster than normal because, duh, they were free, and I wanted to grab another one before intermission was over.

"You'd think I'd be used to this stuff by now, but honestly it's still pretty weird," Bill noted. I agreed about the weirdness factor, but I wasn't complaining—there was an unlimited dessert buffet in front of my face, which I was considering stealthily stuffing into plastic baggies and bringing home in my purse.

That's when I noticed celebrity after celebrity surrounding us in the VIP room. The space was only about one hundred square feet, so everyone was squished into super-close quarters. At one end of the room was Anne Burrell from the Food Network; next to her was the current heavyweight boxing world champion; and across from him was Darryl McDaniels from Run-DMC. Nobody was really socializing, though—everyone seemed oddly bored, and it was not unlike sitting at an empty table at an acquaintance's baby shower in the suburbs.

As we headed back to our seats after intermission, Bill stopped to chat with Tom Hanks, whom he had apparently met before. Suddenly I found myself sandwiched between Bill, Tom, and Brian Williams. I introduced myself, and they gave me their first names, as if I didn't know who they were. Naturally we started talking about hockey, and I took credit for making Bill go to his first game. It was surreal having a ten-minute conversation with every mom's favorite actor, but Tom Hanks turned out to be a totally normal guy and it felt pretty comfortable.

Later that night, Bill and I headed back to his Midtown apartment, which had the shiniest floors I had ever seen. The whole place was pretty fucking clean—especially for a guy's apartment. The view out of the six-foot windows was exceptional, too, of course. I'd been planning on going home, but it was late and Brooklyn was far, and that seemed like a good enough excuse to stay at his place. Plus, I hadn't had sex in six months. Oh, right, I already said that.

Even if I did get to talk hockey with Tom Hanks that night, I knew that Bill's inconsistent communication and lack of excitement toward me pointed to the fact that he wasn't really relationship material. But he was fun to look at, and I was having fun, so I planned to take full advantage of the night ahead of me.

My earlier prediction about his penis size was right, which made my next day wearing dirty clothes somewhat worth it. What possibly made it even more worth it was his extremely comfortable Tempur-Pedic mattress, with linens that were thread count "I have tons of money to spend on really nice sheets." I left early for work, and though he gave me what seemed like a sweet, genuine good-bye and said he wanted to see me again, the only thing I left feeling sure about was that I needed to order new sheets.

THEY REALLY SAID THIS.
PART 17

Are you as interesting as you look?

Nope.

I didn't think so.

Broke

In February 2014, the very same week the *New York* magazine article had boldly dubbed me "the most popular woman on OKCupid," I got fired from my job at a makeup counter.

I admit: Breaking up with Ethan right before Christmas and spending countless long, gray days trekking through the NYC tundra hadn't done wonders for my motivation. My seasonal depression was in full effect, and sleeping all day seemed like a far better way to pass the time than helping indecisive customers pick which shade of nude lipstick they should buy. My attitude then could be best described as "hating abso-fucking-lutely everything," though in my defense, during the month or two leading up to my termination, I'd made a legitimate effort to pull my shit together, and I had—so I wasn't expecting to be fired.

But fired I was, and for a shitty reason. My manager's manager, Justine, had always seemed to misread my occasional quietness as bitchiness, which she expressed to several of my coworkers but not to me. From that point on, I realized Justine was a fifteen-year-old inhabiting a thirty-five-year-old woman's body. I knew I'd be better off without that job and dealing with drama that should exist only in a middle school.

Plus, I'd been working in customer service for almost ten years, and to say it was getting old would be a profound understatement. Getting let go actually felt pretty liberating.

And because the *New York* piece had just come out, I was being approached for tons of new and unfamiliar opportunities. I had plenty of meetings with TV networks wanting me to star in my own reality show, and I did a dozen or so radio interviews for stations across the country. Whether it's being randomly featured in a national magazine or witnessing a man masturbating on a public train, New York City never has a shortage of surprises to offer. Obviously the magazine qualified as a significantly more pleasant one, and though it helped soften the blow of my empty bank account, none of these new offers felt quite right, so I passed on most of them. All the production companies wanting to work with me had interest only in diving headfirst into the details of my dating life. I wasn't ready to hand all my privacy over to a camera crew, and I also didn't want to be known only as a reality star.

After applying for unemployment benefits, I was rewarded with a hefty two hundred dollars per week. Depending on where you live, that may seem like a reasonable amount of cash. It actually averages out to less than ten thousand a year, though, and I live in one of the most expensive cities in the country, so yeah—it sucked. I'm still shocked at how cheap everything is outside of New York City. Going to a bar in suburbia and paying four dollars for a drink or to a grocery store and paying two dollars for toothpaste makes me feel like a queen.

According to one of the 527 documentaries I've watched, I probably would've been better off begging for money at Penn Station than relying on my unemployment check. Unfortunately, I do possess some dignity and do not possess a raging heroin habit, so I stuck with receiving a low-balance alert in my in-box every morning and prayed to the money gods that I wouldn't get charged that much-maligned thirty-five-dollar overdraft fee.

I never understood the "funemployment" term. Receiving a check for not working every week seems like it'd be enjoyable, but in actuality my "job" was now nothing more than looking for a new one. I found a few freelance makeup gigs and even tried bartending at a super-douchey bar. I quickly learned that being sober while flanked by drunk white males in green plaid shorts rapping to Biggie was the exact definition of hell, and no amount of money could have kept me around for that.

Any hope I was holding on to began turning to complete frustration as I applied for literally hundreds of jobs (no, *literally* hundreds) with no luck. The most grating part was that I actually got called back for a good amount of second and third interviews. The rejection emails always read along the lines of, "Lauren, we thought very highly of you, and it was an extremely tough decision, but we are going with another candidate." I even went as far as asking the employers what I could do to improve, and they never gave me negative feedback. So, you're telling me you loved me, my résumé and cover letter were great, but I can't have the job, and you have nothing to tell me about WHY, exactly? Like, shoot me in the fucking face.

It was kind of surreal, having to print out résumés at Staples and hustle across the city on an empty stomach . . . all while receiving tons of fawning calls from producers wanting to create reality shows about my life. All the attention may have looked kind of glamorous from the outside, but nobody realized I hadn't eaten in three days, had to borrow money for my MetroCard, and had turned my apartment upside down searching for quarters. My social life would have been dead if not for good friends—and first dates!—offering to buy me drinks when we went out. Having no financial freedom is miserable, and not all forms of Internet fame pay your rent. I'll admit, I'm jealous of those girls who have enough followers on Instagram to help them get paid to promote a fucking water bottle.

About five months into my jobless crusade with still no steady work, I was depending on unemployment benefits and random freelance jobs. All that disappointment and depression led me to go out and treat my body like shit almost every weekend. My tolerance for alcohol was that of a three-hundred-pound frat boy and putting coke up my nose every weekend didn't seem like a big deal anymore, when previously it . . . had. I'd wake up with the worst hangovers of my life and do it all over again the next day.

It was summer, the time of the year when ten or so of my closest friends and I would rent a weekend house in the Catskills to briefly escape the concrete jungle. I couldn't even buy toilet paper, so naturally I couldn't afford to go on the trip this year, but thankfully Kathleen agreed to pay my way. (I think part of the reason she wanted me to go, however, was so she wouldn't have to be the only single person around four couples.)

Our boozy four-day getaway, complete with the requisite Taylor Swift sing-alongs, was a refreshing break from another disgusting summer in the city, but I couldn't help but think about the financial hole I was still buried in at home. What if I was forced to move back to—*the horror*—my mom's house on Maryland's eastern shore, where the most exciting thing going on was the grand opening of a new Chick-fil-A? The thought of being surrounded by people who think red lipstick is wild and racism doesn't exist was enough to distract me from the fun time I should've been having.

On our last day there, the stress of the past few months hit me like a ton of bricks, and out of nowhere I started tearing up in the middle of a game of Cards Against Humanity. I crept off to the bathroom, where I bawled more than I had in ages. In fact, I hadn't cried so hard since being dumped the year before; my strong-woman shell was clearly starting to shatter under pressure. I felt pathetic for borrowing money from Kathleen and for hardly being able to cover my rent for the past six months, plus I was extremely pissed that all my efforts to find a job weren't paying off in the slightest. I sat on the toilet for a while and waited for my eyes to stop looking like I'd just smoked five blunts before heading back downstairs to join the obnoxious card game.

Almost at my breaking point, it seems my wishes had finally been granted—or something—when, out of nowhere, I started receiving call after call about possible jobs. All of the networking and emails I had sent out were starting to pay off. My freelance makeup gigs picked up, and I had an interview with a new startup company that would wind up ultimately changing my life. Thanks to Kelli, the now-friend who hired me, I would quickly rack up a list of celebrity clientele and get tons of ridiculous opportunities. Finally, my input was respected, being myself was what got me ahead, and for the first time, "work" didn't feel like work.

My blog also started getting more notice, and I attracted the attention of a literary agent. She would eventually help me get the deal that led to the book you're holding in your hands this very second. It all felt crazy, but fitting at the same time. I was twenty-four, ambitious, and I finally felt like I was being recognized for that—like I was strong enough to accomplish things most people see as unreachable in a city that tears people down every day.

like a unicorn sliding down a rainbow into a pot of honey but the honey isn't sticky when it come out cuz u r so fucking sexy u make honey lose its stickiness . . .

Now Hiring:
Part-Time Boyfriend

Thank you for your interest in the position of "part-time boyfriend." Please see below for a job description.

Responsibilities:

Take me to various places

Produce intelligent conversation

Keep consistently exceptional personal hygiene

Be great at sex

Listen to my random thoughts

Give me compliments

Tolerate my passion for E! and Bravo

Requirements:

A genuine personality

At least five years experience in similar work

Comfort with who you are as a person

Knowledge and usage of basic grammar

Must love animals, especially my cat, Meemow

If selected for the position, benefits and perks include:

Omelets in the morning

Support and motivation

Someone to travel with

Thoughtful gifts for no reason

A movie-watching buddy

A real-life vagina (not a photo of one on the Internet)

Someone who will listen to you complain

Boobs you are allowed to touch

While this is currently just a part-time position, if you show great enthusiasm and don't act like a psycho, there is definite room for growth.

Red Flags to Ignore at Your Own Peril

Ever been on what you thought was a perfect first date, all glow-y and shiny and full of promise for your shared romantic future? Ever continue dating that person, even as more and more nagging little warning signs began popping up—tiny clues that the dude you were so excited about is actually, well, very wrong for you? We've all been there, but before you keep blindly soldiering forward and ignoring the hints—hoping against hope that somehow your gut will turn out to be wrong, just this once—take note of a few of the more common red flags it would behoove you not to ignore.

He talks about an ex in a message OR on a first date.

Exes are off-limits as conversation topics until you've been dating for a solid while. Why? Because nobody wants to hear intimate details of a guy's sordid romantic past, and the more he talks about her, the more glaringly obvious it is that what's past isn't actually past. If he's talking about her, he's not over her—end of story. Get out now.

He calls said ex(es) "crazy."

We've all heard this one, but trust me, it's a bad sign. Ending relationships on sour, bitter notes happens to the best of us from time to time, but it's generally not something you want to broadcast to potential partners. Calling your exes names makes YOU seem like the asshole, and it's just all-around disrespectful. If a dude starts pulling the "she's crazy" card, consider what he might say about you six months down the line, and think about moving along.

He's a Peter Pan type.

Anyone who lives in a big city like NYC or LA is familiar with the phenomenon known as Peter Pan Syndrome— guys in their late twenties, thirties, and up who'd prefer to *play*, for the rest of their lives, instead of growing the fuck up like the normal humans around them. Guys aren't usually aware of this issue in themselves, but their inner PP problem is readily apparent without words. If he's never (or rarely) been in a relationship; chronically seeks "casual sex" or "short-term dating;" moves around a ton and never seems to settle in one place for more than a year; has no interest in marriage, kids, or home ownership; or has an annoying young-person job at a flashy tech startup, beware.

He disappears between dates.

I once dated a guy who seemed great in nearly every way—he was kind, hot, and all over me with affection whenever we'd get together once or twice a week. The problem? In between those dates, he'd vanish without a trace—no contact for days and days. His mysterious absence made me increasingly anxious, which led to me feeling like I had to constantly reach out to him if I wanted to see him, which seemed to make him less and less interested in seeing me at all. If he's interested in you only when he's physically with you, it's safe to assume he's just in it for the action; it might be time to walk away.

He doesn't like—or seems apathetic about—animals.

As a lover of any and all animals, it's a screaming red flag to me if a guy doesn't seem into them. What's not to like? They're cute, cuddly, fur-covered creatures that offer unconditional love and acceptance. Plus, they're pretty much helpless (at least our pets are) and they depend on us for food, shelter, and survival. A guy who doesn't dig pets is a guy that doesn't seem nurturing or compassionate and doesn't seem to give a damn about helping the underdog (ha ha). And those qualities are generally not things I'm looking for in a man.

He doesn't care about meeting your friends (or having you meet his).

If I'm dating a guy for more than a couple of months and he makes no move to introduce me to his friends—or, worse, he has no interest in meeting mine—it's a pretty obvious no-go flag. I dated a guy who would bail every time I tried to set up a time for him to hang with my family or friends. The relationship didn't go much further due to him cheating on me (see, I told you, red flag).

He's rude to strangers.

We've all heard the one about being wary of people who are rude to waitstaff. But I'd like to expand that maxim to being rude to strangers in general. A guy who doesn't take the time to be decent to cashiers, taxi drivers, or even randoms on the street just can't be trusted to be kind to you. Of course, I live in New York, where life is fast-moving and people don't always have time to be all *Kumbaya* with each other, but there's something to be said for basic civility and respect. And neither of them should be hard.

He won't admit to being wrong. Ever.

There's almost nothing more frustrating than getting into an argument with a guy who refuses to admit when he's, well, totally wrong. Every time I've dated a dude like that, things inevitably didn't end well. That kind of stubbornness, to me, also connotes arrogance, self-importance, defensiveness, and a lack of generosity, none of which are particularly appealing traits in a potential mate.

hey beautfuil lovey to meet u my name is george aka jorge del bloque or jorgy boy but I have to say god blesss u sweety u r something elsee u are and angel

In his defense, maybe he grew up on a planet where grammar didn't exist.

Marriage & Kids (or the Lack Thereof)

I n middle school, I was completely sure I never wanted a husband or kids.

My twelve-year-old self just didn't buy the marriage thing. If you loved someone, why would you need a piece of paper to define what you were? My parents had just divorced, and I never wanted to go through that shit myself. The endless screaming in the kitchen every night as I tried to fall asleep was loud, grating— the opposite of Nickelodeon. And as for kids, I had too much to do, too much life ahead of me, to even haltingly consider the idea of being responsible for a small, dependent human. "Just wait till you get older. You'll change your mind," everyone kept assuring me.

When I was fifteen, my views did change a bit, thanks to Matt, one of the very first guys to make me cry. He broke up with me via AOL Instant Messenger after a whole month because he "didn't want a girlfriend." He was three years older than me, had introduced me to his parents, and I'd even had sex with him, so I was pretty much devastated when it ended. I was sure I'd never date someone so good-looking and put-together again. Over the years, of course, Matt would become unattractive, and I'd learn that guys would tell you whatever they thought you wanted to hear if it would advance their cause of using their penis for something other than peeing and masturbating.

While Matt and my other first few mini-breakups sucked, having actual feelings for dudes did prompt me to start reevaluating why it might actually, possibly, maybe, one day, be a fathomable idea for two people to get betrothed to each other. However, I determined that if I did sell out and succumb to the societal norm, I'd wear a red dress at my future wedding. I'd be SO unique and not like all the other women in their generic white dresses.

Then, when I was seventeen, I fell in love for the first time. I couldn't imagine being with anyone but Christian—who, as you remember, I ended up dating for four long years—and as my style evolved, white lace started to look kind of . . . pretty.

My mom still gives me shit for saying I never wanted to get married. I understand where twelve-year-old Lauren was coming from, though. Since my parents' long-ago split, I've seen countless other friends' and family members' marriages fall apart. The origin of the practice really doesn't lend a helping hand to why I'd choose to get married, either, and I think doing anything for the sake of tradition is quite dumb. These days, I have other reasons for why I'd consider tying the knot, although I probably wouldn't have any type of traditional ceremony, if I had one at all. I haven't changed my mind about not wanting kids, though, and while my mom has accepted that, I still get annoyed when strangers seem to get off on telling me that I'll change my mind.

For me, marriage and giving birth to small beings who run around and knock shit over don't necessarily go hand in hand. Plus, I have a cat if I want to see my shit get knocked off a table. Kids are good for some things, like making people feel bad for you when there are no seats on the subway, or teaching you the delicate art of strong-armed manipulation (fine, *maybe* they could help some people figure out how to be slightly less selfish assholes, too), but they're far from the only reason to get married. I have four nieces and nephews that I love to pieces when they're not screaming about nothing, but when they are, I'm allowed to leave straightaway without later getting hunted down by Child Protective Services, and I value that. I also simply enjoy my freedom—waking up when I want, booking a flight to another country when I want—and I don't believe that pushing a human being out of my vagina is the only way I'll live a fulfilled, happy life. Traveling the world, experiencing new cultures, falling in love, making a difference, and taking care of five puppies also sound pretty damn great to me.

I've gotten the impression from lots of people, though, that there's "no point" in getting married if you don't want kids. While marriage traditions have obviously varied throughout history depending on geography, and cultural and religious stuff, to me, marriage is nothing more than a formal union between two people who love each other and want that commitment to be recognized legally and socially. However great polyandry (when a woman is married to more than one man—you go, lady) may be, I want only one guy around to harass about wiping his piss off the toilet seat. Besides the obvious tax benefits, though, demonstrating such a firm commitment to someone kind of warms my heart in its simplicity, as does having the balls to proudly declare how much bullshit AND amazingness you're willing to endure alongside a partner.

All in all, I'm like lots of women in that I want to be inspired by whoever I'm with, and I want to support them in whatever endeavors they take on. I see a life partner as someone I never have to protect myself around, someone I feel comfortable with, even when my eyebrows aren't filled in. If a dysfunctional couple who has broken up five times already *and* had a kid unexpectedly can get married without being questioned, I should be able to get married, for love and love alone, without being interrogated about the no-kids thing.

Still, though, I have my moments of wondering whether monogamy is even . . . natural. It can be hard to believe in it sometimes when I've witnessed so much disloyalty in relationships every single day. I've been cheated on in two of my past relationships, and I can't even count how many times I've been approached by guys who had girlfriends or wives. Just two days ago, in fact, I was doing makeup on a woman in her hotel room. She was getting ready to go to her son's wedding in the city and as soon as I finished and she walked away, her husband started openly flirting with me.

And, though I've never cheated myself, toward the end of my relationship with Christian, I felt so emotionally and physically unfulfilled that I *wanted* to pursue someone else—a man who would unquestioningly give me the attention Christian suddenly refused to. I broke up with him instead of going there, but at that point I truly understood how that desire to stray can come up—how a need for affection can get the best of us. To me that doesn't mean monogamy isn't natural, though; it just means it sucks to be ignored by the person you love.

Plus, if monogamy isn't innately ingrained, why do we get so crazy when it comes to keeping our partners solely to ourselves? We'd all be in open relationships or living like the fucking TLC sister-wives if we didn't exhibit tendencies for possessiveness and exclusivity. Extreme jealousy and possessiveness suck, to be sure, but in some ways they seem expected, even natural.

In any case, we're all constantly evolving, and whether we're able to keep up with our partners' evolution plays a huge role in determining how successful our monogamous relationships—and our marriages—end up being. I can't even comprehend how my parents were married for eleven years when they're such demonstrably different people with pretty much nothing in common. Obviously dedication and passion have to exist in a successful marriage, but I can't help think that maybe the couples who last a lifetime just got lucky, that they happened to grow in the same direction, at the same pace.

Monogamy, whether ultimately "natural" or not, only feels right to me when I'm with someone I truly love and see a legit future with. As Justin Timberlake has bravely sung, "I got that tunnel vision for you." Just let me know when you're finally talking to me, Justin.

I'd soOo eat u out ;)

I'd soOo decline that offer.

Catfished

You know that show *Catfish*? (I know you do, so don't bother pretending you're above watching stupid shit on MTV.) It's a great representation of what happens every day online, and it's probably gained such insane popularity in the past couple years not just because it's extremely entertaining to watch awkward dorks who sit behind their computer all day get blindsided by massive cameras, but because it could happen to anyone who uses Internet dating sites.

What some naysayers find bizarre about the *Catfish* premise is the idea two people could fall in legitimate love (or misguidedly *think* they've fallen in their own pseudo-kinda-maybe-love) without ever having met in person. We've all been irritated by that Boston-based friend of a friend who changed her Facebook status to "in a relationship" with some military-recruit Iowan she's been chatting with for all of three months (and yes, OF COURSE they're planning on meeting in person! Maybe even next week, if he can get his mom's car!). Not only is it weird to change your status for someone you've never physically met, but I also don't understand the point of communicating endlessly with someone who lives one thousand miles away. Bad prognosis much?

As wacky as it sounds, though, the notion of falling for someone you've never technically laid in-person eyes on is weird only to the lucky few who have never tried looking for love in the virtual realm. The millions of us doing the online-dating dance aren't doing it for our health—we're doing it because we're looking for a real connection. Internet dating can make finding those connections seem just a tiny bit easier, at least on the surface.

Having the ability to literally filter the people you'll deign to lay eyes on according to their religion, height, and drinking habits can lull some people into thinking they've found their "perfect match" a little too easily. But keeping a clear mind and maintaining some skepticism about that super-attractive guy who claims to make a shit ton of money *and* own a golden retriever puppy is a smart idea.

What this all means? Some online relationships can be based on the foundational equivalent of horseshit. Take the woman who knowingly passes herself off as her best friend's hot sister, or the forty-something guy who says he's mid-divorce when in reality he's been married for twenty years and his wife has nary a clue that the reason his iPhone dies by noon every day is because it's overstuffed with hookup apps.

Luckily my cynicism has served me well, and I've never been caught up in an online love affair based on lies. But nobody ever really talks about the folks on the other end of the catfishing spectrum—the ones who find their photos attached to the hcious profile of some aging, Midwestern goat farmer claiming to be twenty-four, single, and living it up in Bushwick. And yeah, that's actually happened to me: on multiple occasions, a friend—or just some random person on the Internet—has emailed me a screenshot of someone pretending to be me on OKCupid, Instagram, or *insert favorite dating site here*.

I try to see it as a compliment, but it's actually pretty annoying, not to mention creepy. I feel a bit violated knowing that someone's using my photos to talk to people online while the person they are talking to has no idea it's not actually them. The first time it happened, one of my blog followers sent me the user's OKCupid profile that claimed I lived in Iowa and "just wanted a guy to cuddle with." I sent a message to the supposed "me" saying "I don't actually want a guy to just cuddle with and you should probably delete this profile." It was deleted the next day.

Various versions of me out there have been thirty-three, avid smokers, "luv getting tatz," and looking ONLY for polyam-orous relationships. What bothered me most, though, on a few of my impersonators' profiles? But of course! It was their painfully incorrect usage of "your" vs. "you're."

If you stay smart about it, though, you can (hopefully) avoid getting catfished. If you're not so lucky—or if you feel like there's a smidgen of a chance that your perfect faraway dream lover might be a slightly less-than-perfect faraway match, keep reading. They're probably faking it—or hiding something big—if . . .

They won't video chat you.

If they won't let you see their real, live, talking and smiling face, they're keeping something from you . . . that something being the way they, like, *actually look*. RUN.

They won't meet you in person.

If they keep making excuses about why they can't meet up, again, they're holding something back—maybe they actually are who they say they are, but a two-hundred-pound-heavier or married version.

They ask you for money.

Don't be stupid. Please.

They have no online or social-media presence other than the spot where you met them.

If there's nothing to back up who they are on the Internet—whether it be a Google search or Instagram, Twitter, or LinkedIn accounts—they're most likely making something up.

They look a little too familiar.

If you think you might have seen them before, well, you really might have; they could be using random models' photos (or they could be using photos of random people like me!).

They come on super-strong, super-fast.

If they're making grand proclamations about how incredible you are after knowing you for two weeks, pull a ghost on them—this would definitely fall under the "too-good-to-be-true" category.

It's Not Just Me: Kim, 29

Ahoyyy!" My phone screen lit up with a curiously piratic greeting. I groaned as I read the rest of the long-winded text message from the latest Match suitor whom I had yet to meet.

I'd begun talking to the pirate approximately a week prior, and despite being overly enthusiastic in his emails—not to mention responding to all of mine merely minutes after I had pressed reply—he gave me no cause for concern. Well, other than the fact that his profile stated his height was five foot six (I feared even shorter) and that he had potentially dangerous sideburns.

Yet I decided to give him the benefit of the doubt. Maybe he had just watched *Hook* (Dustin Hoffman was pretty badass).

I swallowed my pride and drove to the location of our drinks date after work. As I approached the restaurant, a squat, baseball-cap-wearing figure came into view, and it took all I could do not to turn and run. Jack Sparrow was approximately my height—five foot four—with full-on mutton chops that triggered my gag reflex. As I struggled to reach a shaky hand toward him, he began to speak. "Hey, how's it goinghrmrmhrm." Come again, Mumbles?

As we entered the restaurant, we were seated at a booth and perused the menu while we placed our drink orders. "So, were you planning on getting anything to eat?" I asked.

"Oh, no, I'm not really hungry. I got a really bad case of food poisoning last night," he said, trailing off into a deranged mumble-laugh hybrid. A seasick pirate? Be still my beating heart.

The wine started to kick in. As Blackbeard droned on about how his band once played at a Bickford's restaurant, declared that he absolutely hated my favorite local pub–trivia spot, and expressed his genuine surprise that he didn't know anyone at the restaurant tonight (he's kind of a big deal in the Boston suburbs), my increasingly glazed-over gaze wandered to the unused salad fork on my left. Wasn't he supposed to be getting better as I drank?

Realizing that I'd completely checked out of the one-sided conversation by then, I tuned in briefly to catch " . . . and we have a pool at my house."

I feigned interest: "You live with roommates?"

He bristled. "At my house, actually. I live at home. With my parents." Easy there, tiger!

Accepting defeat, I chugged the rest of my Riesling as he began to jokingly gripe about how his mother thinks he's a functioning alcoholic. So what if he likes to only drink after work? Every day? And while gambling at Foxwoods every weekend with his "boys"? What does she expect him to do, sit around and read books? "Oh, sorry," he muttered. "You're in a book club, right?"

Smee rose abruptly. "I'm going to the bathroom," he

declared. Saved by the bladder! Still mumblechuckling, he continued. "If you're not here when I get back, I'll understand!" Apparently my bitch vibes were more potent than I realized.

I probably should have hightailed it out of there, but I breathed a sigh of relief as the check came and he did one thing right: swiping it out of my sight as I did the ol' purse reach. "What kind of fool do you take me for?" he guffawed.

"Uh . . . "

Hey, you are cute, little mouse. Wanna play a game? And no, before you start insinuating, it's not sexual, you perv.

Too Many Fucking Dating Sites

T here are almost too many dating sites these days, and while some have obvious differences, like JDate and ChristianMingle, not all of them are so easily deciphered, and they can get overwhelming. I think lots of people in my age range end up opting for OKCupid because it doesn't cost anything and it attracts mostly twenty- and thirtysomethings. However, being free makes it kind of a free-for-all, and as my blog proves, you'll probably get messaged by creeps of all kinds. For those reasons, I've broken down some of the top sites and apps out there right now.

Let's go in descending order of Seriousness, with #5 being super-conservative marriage-minded-like-whoa, and #1 being "Yo, let's hook up."

5. EHARMONY

T his should come as no surprise. eHarmony has long been held up as the go-to site for straight (and straight-only!) folks who are taking Internet dating SERIOUSLY—like, bridal veil, picket fence, SUV, and twin-boys-named-Ashton seriously. It's owned by an elderly white Christian man, Neil Clark Warren, who in 2000 founded the company with a little help from Focus on the

Family, a "Christian values" nonprofit. The site has been widely and rightfully bashed for not deigning to match nonhetero couples, though it did launch a sister site called Compatible Partners for gay peeps (how sweet of them!). This site is worthless for edgy types, creatives, or hipsters—it's basically the anti-OKCupid.

4. MATCH

Match is way less conservative-Bible-intense than eHarmony but much classier than OKCupid. Like eHarmony, it's a paid thing, so the thirty-five million people who are there (!) actually want to be there, which I think indicates a higher quality pool as far as the guys being invested in legit relationships. Of course, this doesn't mean finding an awesome dude is any easier there than anywhere else—one of my friends tried Match and said the few guys she met were about as "beige" as they come (aka boring, basic, blah). But if you're looking for a real relationship with a steady guy, Match might be for you.

3. PLENTYOFFISH

Plentyoffish, like OKCupid, is free, which makes it appealing to a range of users—twenty-three million of them, to be precise. But who exactly those twenty-three million people are is beyond me, because I've never seen, spoken to, or heard of any of them. For some reason I associate this site with the Midwest, even the Bible Belt; people who have never met anyone from the Internet before a friend convinced them to try it. Then they dutifully Googled "online dating" and signed up with the first site that popped up. One thing about POF, though, is that it bans folks from seeking only casual flings or May-December romances, so I guess that's cool if you're looking for something more solid.

2. OKCUPID, HAPPN, and HINGE

All three of these online dating options can really go either way. They all don't cost a thing and for the most part are youth-oriented (at least that's how it's always seemed throughout my tons and tons of unofficial research), so there are lots of millennials looking to have fun and—let's be frank—get laid. Of course there are relationship-seekers there, too, but you never really know what someone's intentions are because it's such a hodgepodge.

These sites and apps are great for people who are kind of just down for whatever. Personally, I don't NEED a partner but if someone awesome came along, I'd be open to a serious relationship. I can always open up one of these apps and arrange a date if I want to, but I'm not paying for a membership, so I don't feel like I HAVE TO use them. And while there are tons of guys online who are looking only to fuck as many girls as possible, that doesn't mean success stories never happen—I know more than a handful of great couples who met on OKCupid, including some who wound up getting married.

1. TINDER

Tinder started out feeling icky, like Grindr for straight kids—a superficial app to facilitate meaningless hookups and little more. The basis of only deciding if you "like" someone by seeing a couple photos and reading almost no text is about as shallow as it gets. But over time it's grown into something more women are using, and more often I'm hearing, "Oh, I met my SO on Tinder."

Once you've crossed that initial looks-based hump, you're free to take the connection further and see if anything is actually there.

City vs. Suburban Dating

Igrew up in an unexceptional Maryland suburb outside DC, where McDonald's and strip malls line the highways; matching your shirt *exactly* to your shoes is perceived as the pinnacle of style; and plenty of people I knew ended up automatically marrying the first person they lost their virginity to.

I go back to visit family every few months, and not surprisingly, each and every time, absolutely nothing has changed. Except for the thrill of the occasional fucking McDonald's PlayPlace renovation or some new roadside condo construction, most people there are content with their nine-to-fives and their wall-to-wall-carpeted domestic lives with fiancés who have already dated three of their friends.

Even though I lived in the same state my whole life, it never felt fully like home. I knew from a young age that I'd want to escape to a bigger, more exciting, slightly less carpeted locale as soon as I turned eighteen. And I did just that, which means I've never really experienced grown-up dating anywhere except

NYC—which is, of course, vastly different from dating in a small town or suburb.

Options (and Lack of Them)

I have a few friends back home who have been with the same guy since high school. Yes, they're my friends and I respect what makes them happy, but I would probably stab myself in the neck if I had only been with one penis my whole life. Maybe these friends got lucky and their relationships were all mystically "meant to be" or whatever, though I can't help but wonder if people like that just stick with what they know because it's safe and comfortable.

I understand the pressure to follow the socially constructed formula of relationship + marriage + steady job + baby = happiness. But thinking about settling for—or settling down with—the first guy I had sex with just because it's What Everyone Says I'm Supposed to Do makes me cringe.

Of course, "settling" seems even more common in suburbia because there's simply less exposure to new things, ideas, and, most importantly, people. When you're starving, you'll kinda eat anything, right?

Population

NYC has about eight million residents; my hometown has around twenty thousand. I probably met, saw, or went to school with literally just about every guy my age back home, while I see hundreds—if not thousands—of new faces every single day in New York. The sheer number of options for males and females in my current city is insanity. This can be simultaneously the best thing and most mortifying thing about dating in a metropolis like mine: Because there are so many single folks, people think they can pick and choose at their discretion. Guys here—and plenty of girls, too—think they're swimming in options, which makes all of us less likely to just sit down, stop fucking swiping left for two secs, and *pick someone* to take to sushi or whatever. It doesn't have to be such a huge ordeal, you guys. Really, it doesn't.

The Disappearing Act

Breakups are hellish no matter where you live, but their logistics get slightly more complicated when you live in a small town. There's that whole awkward running-into-your-ex-at-inopportune-times situation, which obviously happens far more often in the burbs. When your social and cultural outlets pretty much extend as far as one Starbucks, one movie theater, one Chili's, and one sports bar, it's pretty damn likely you won't be able to hide from the girl you dated for four years or the idiot who dumped you via text message.

In New York and other big cities, if you don't run in the same friend circles as your ex, you pretty much never need to worry about bumping into him again, unless you want to. Dating in big cities reigns supreme in this arena—it's so much easier to pretend that someone you fucked no longer even exists. Plus, you have tons of new prospects to scope on the street while you're recovering from what's-his-name.

Personality

When it comes to what people are *actually like*, though, I won't lie: City dating can be rough. Guys in NYC—at least the ones

I've encountered—tend to be much less humble and genuine than dudes in smaller towns. They can also be impossibly shallow and judgmental, expecting the world, even when they've got the opposite of the world to offer. I'm a woman, so my perspectives on NYC ladies are slightly biased, but I think the women here have it way worse dating-wise than the men.

Even though people in the burbs might tend to stick with what they know instead of expanding their horizons, in some ways, smaller-town folks feel, to me, like they're more authentic, more true to themselves. They're not as demanding or judgmental when it comes to love. Hey, is there anything wrong with wanting nothing more than a kind, decent cuddle buddy to cozy up to and watch *Breaking Bad* with on a random Sunday night? If so, then we're all in trouble.

Schedules

In the suburbs, there's one general way to live. It looks a little something like this: You get up at 6:00 AM, you kiss your sleeping hubby/fiancé/partner/whoever, you work out on your elliptical in the basement at a quiet enough volume so as not to wake the fam. Then you shower, eat, and drive off to a job you vaguely despise at an office adjacent to a megaplex, where you stare resentfully at your computer for eight hours from a gray, windowless cubicle.

I am exaggerating, yes. But the truth is that tons of folks in the burbs really *do* live a lifestyle marked by nine-to-five-ish office jobs and all the often-heinous rigmarole that goes along with them. One upside to that? It makes dating pretty easy as far as scheduling goes.

Shit gets trickier in the city, where it seems like only 30 percent of the population works a classic desk job with a computer, a cube, and a preset daily schedule. In NY, we're awash in artists, authors, store clerks, therapists, bike messengers, and whatever else you could possibly dream of (yup, there are plenty of stockbrokers, accountants, and lawyers thrown in there, too). This doesn't make us cooler—believe me, the rat race is painfully alive and well here. And all of the freelance weirdos with their odd hours and unconventional jobs make squeezing in dates tough.

Age

My friends back home who are twenty-five and up are pretty much all hitched, and I can't quite imagine what they'd do if they were suddenly forced to fly solo again—suicide seems like the only option. (I kid, of course—they should just join me in New York!)

Dating in big cities isn't such a huge ordeal for older folks, though. I mean, sure, the available-prospect pool starts draining past age thirty-five no matter where you live. But the sheer number of unattached people of all ages here in NYC makes it feel more likely that anyone could potentially find someone here.

My single New York friends in their late thirties and up have no trouble getting dates on Match or OKC; whether those turn into legit relationships is another story, but whatever. We all need to get out and meet up with someone we haven't already tried to date a year prior, even if it doesn't lead to a floofy white dress, veil, and blood diamond.

can you chat right now . . . I want to tell
you about how im going to spoil you a lot

hey but you may be open to taking cash?

totally can meet with you first but will
you listen to my proposal?

maybe you prefer a different chat but
do you have a secto chat about that
scenario? I am offering you a lot ok??

lets at least chat to try to work
something out between us

Dating on Camera

One night a few months back, I randomly decided to check my "other" in-box on Facebook. You know, the one with all the messages from folks who aren't your actual friends (aka all those creepsters from faraway time zones). This time, surprisingly, I spotted a message from a non-creepster: a smiley blonde named Amy who said she was a recruiter for a new reality dating show on a major network—a show I'd seen ads for splashed across every subway station in NYC.

Amy had found me through the *New York* magazine article, and she said she wanted to set up a time to talk. This wasn't the first time I'd been approached for a TV thing, and I knew for something to actually come to fruition, it would take tons of time plus a shitload of back-and-forth with producers, assistants, assistants' assistants, interns, interns' interns, and whoever else would be involved in the spectacle.

I was a bit uncertain—I'd turned down several reality offers in months prior. Being portrayed as something I'm not *or* forever being seen as just another dried-up "reality star" didn't exactly sound enticing to me. Plus, working as a makeup artist and having tons of friends in the business, I was well aware that reality shows were anything but real. One producer actually wanted me to go on thirty dates in thirty days with thirty different guys. And not just that—each date had to cost less than thirty dollars. That many awkward forced outings with no alcohol (or, alternately, really cheap/awful alcohol) and shitty food would have scarred me for life.

For some reason, though, I was intrigued by this Amy person's email, and we arranged a call for the next morning. The second episode of this particular dating show was actually on that night, so of course I tuned in. This was actually one of the first reality shows of its kind. It was filmed in real time in NYC week by week, with each episode airing the following week. There were two straight guys, one gay guy, and two straight women all looking for love. They'd each go on a new date every week, with viewers giving them advice via social media. The show had already been underway for two weeks, and Amy thought I could be perfect as one of the guys' potential dates.

Watching the show, I didn't have high expectations for the two straight men on it. I expected them to be typical cheeseball dating-show bros. You know, classically good-looking but firmly devoid of brains, with no legit interest in anything but chicks, kegs, *Monday Night Football*, and boat shoes. Interestingly, though, one of them did catch my attention.

I wasn't initially physically attracted to Ryan—at least not the way he looked on TV—but he had style and seemed confident and intelligent. The cool thing about this particular show, I learned, was that all the cast members seemed like actual people I'd see out and about in New York. They weren't, like, manufactured Snooki clones—they were all just normal, successful people who were, like me, frustrated with trying to find a real connection in this impossible city.

That night, I watched this Ryan dude go on a date with some girl from Staten Island. She thoroughly fulfilled the borough's stereotype in every possible way. She was heavily accented; fake-tanned to the point of looking like an orange; wearing an ill-fitting, cheap floral dress; and her dark roots dipped four inches into her brassy, bleached hair. The date went from bad to worse as she drank a few too many glasses of chardonnay and kept exclaiming how "FUNNN!!!" she was. He wasn't having it, and it was pretty comical how closely my reactions matched his every time she did yet another over-the-top stupid thing. It was kind of surreal to think that I might soon be following in her (humiliating?) footsteps on national television.

During our call the next morning, Amy asked me to make a minute-long video that would "really show off my personality." After taking an hour to decide what to wear and another hour getting my hair and makeup all perfecto, I spent at least another damn hour immersed in Photo Booth on my computer, redoing my silly clip a trillion times. "HEY GUYS! My name is Lauren, and I'm a makeup artist, and I wanna date Ryan because . . ."

I thought I sounded insipid, but I sent the video off anyway, and a couple days later Amy invited me to the show's office to talk to producers. I felt pretty good, having already done several of these types of reality-show meetings before. I clicked immediately with Bryan and Sarah, two of the execs, and before I left, I

signed my life away on a release form. *Ryan, get ready, I'm a-comin'*
for you! I thought self-assuredly. (OK, maybe that's not *exactly*
what I thought, but it was something like that.)

Then things got . . . irritating. For the next five weeks, every
week like clockwork, Bryan or Sarah would call and excitedly tell
me that I'd DEFINITELY be shooting a date with Ryan THAT
VERY WEEK. And every single time, either the day before or
the day of the supposed date, Bryan or Sarah would call me last-
minute and claim there was a change of plans. I couldn't help but
feel frustrated. By then, I was watching the show every week, and
oddly, I was starting to feel like I was truly getting to *know* this
dude. By that point I didn't give a shit about being on TV—I
just genuinely wanted to meet Ryan. Instead, the producers kept
setting him up with losers. One week it was a bland, polyamorous
hippie chick; another week, an egocentric pastor's daughter who
was saving herself for marriage. Uh, no.

There were only a couple of episodes left in the season, so
after being strung along for weeks, I finally gave up on the idea
of meeting Ryan in person OR appearing on the show . . . until I
got another phone call.

"We want you to do a speed-dating thing with Ryan. Are
you available this Friday?" Bryan asked breathlessly. "We want
you and a few other girls to do mini ten-minute dates with him.
He hasn't had much luck on the show so far."

I was less than enthused, assuming they'd call me later that
week and bail again. Still, Ryan . . .

"Are you absolutely sure I won't be canceled on?"

"Positive."

Two days later, I threw on a leather jacket, black pencil skirt, and red lipstick. The two months of anticipation leading up to that night had probably made me more nervous than I ordinarily would've been, so I met up with my friend Shawnte for a drink beforehand to calm my nerves. The minutes dragged like hours as I waited for six o'clock to close in. I felt completely out of my comfort zone.

Not surprisingly, when I called one of the producers to let them know I'd arrived, they said they were running behind schedule. They told me to hang out there and they'd let me know when they were ready. Already having waited sooooo long to do this and growing increasingly annoyed by the millisecond, I was nearly ready to go home, put on sweatpants and write the whole situation off. Instead, Shawnte and I ordered another glass of wine.

Out of the corner of my eye, I saw Bryan walk into the restaurant, five girls trailing behind him. They were clearly the other five chicks who would be speed dating with me. Obviously I needed to scope out how hot (or, um, un-hot) the other girls were, but the only one in my view was wearing a fishnet, see-through shirt and cotton-candy-pink lipstick. I sighed in relief and hoped the other girls looked equally tragic. Bryan spotted me across the room and came to update me on the situation.

"It's most likely going to be around nine or ten when we need you," he informed me.

"So . . . why was I told to be here at six?"

Bryan apologized for the shitty schedule and told us to order whatever we wanted; the network would pick up the tab.

A couple drinks in, one of the girls sitting at the other table walked over. Before introducing herself, she announced, "So Bryan said you were also waiting to be called in, and I just had to say hi because my best friend would absolutely *love you*. You totally need to meet him."

"Oh?" Caught off guard, I actually starting laughing. This whole night was getting stranger and stranger.

"So you're here for the show, too?" I asked the outgoing blonde, whose name was Crystal.

"Yep, but I'm about to fucking leave if they don't call me in right this second. I have to take my dog out. I don't even want to be here; my friend who works on the show begged me to do it because they knew I'd act crazy."

That's when I realized I was the only girl there that genuinely wanted to meet Ryan. Everyone else just wanted their shot on TV—surprise, surprise.

A flash went off in my face as Crystal asked too late, "Can I take a picture of you to send to my friend?"

"Let me see him. What's his name?"

"Ben," she said, scrolling through Instagram. I glanced at her phone as she pulled up a pic from a few weeks earlier.

"Whoa, he looks familiar," I noted, trying to figure out where I had seen him before. I couldn't put my finger on it. Maybe OKCupid? Still, he was pretty attractive, and she kept raving about how great he was.

"OK, just give him my Instagram—'LoandtheCosmos'—there's more than enough pictures there."

She repeated, "LoandtheCosmos? Wait . . . You went on a date with him already! I remember him talking about you! It was, like, a year ago? You went to some bar in Brooklyn?"

The memory flashed back, and once again I realized how bizarro this night was getting.

Over the next couple hours, Shawnte and I started mingling with the girls waiting at the other table. I didn't have anything in common with them, but I was curious to know how everyone else had ended up there. One of the girls was contacted by the show's producers via Twitter, and one had a blog they'd found her through—it documented her life as a virgin.

One by one, as the hours rolled on, each remaining girl got plucked by producers to walk across the street to the filming location until it was just me, Shawnte, and the girl with that tragic fishnet shirt. I was glad Shawnte had stayed for moral support so I didn't have to force a conversation with this thirty-five-year-old from Jersey who was willingly bedecked in gross juniors' clothing.

Finally, Bryan showed up to announce that it was my turn. Ryan was sitting in a clothing store across the street with his back facing the front door. When producers signaled, I would walk in and introduce myself. I started to immediately regret the few glasses of wine I'd had. I wasn't drunk, but I definitely wasn't sober. I started to sweat and could only imagine how red my face looked. I got a nod from a producer and opened the door. My heels clicking on the wood floor was the only thing I heard as the twenty people in production silently stared at me.

"Hi, I'm Lauren," I said as I hugged this random, cute-ish dude I'd watched as he dated on TV for the past few months.

The next thirty minutes were nothing short of the most awkward experience of my entire life. It wasn't awkward because Ryan and I didn't get along. He was nice, witty, and smart, and I thought we had some chemistry. It was awkward because sitting under hot lights with a heap of strangers staring at you and critiquing every word you say is . . . insanity. I would say something.

Then a producer would immediately ask me to repeat it in a different way. I would sit one way, and they'd tell me to pose at a different angle. Nothing about the experience was natural; that half hour was a complete blur. I wasn't being myself—the producers wouldn't let me—so things didn't end up going any further with Ryan.

A few days later, the episode aired. I wasn't on it. Production wound up cutting the speed-dating scenes in their entirety, and despite all the time I wasted, I'm actually super-grateful that my uncomfortable, half-drunk self didn't end up a potential laughing stock on national television. Thanks, "reality"!

I'd love to sit knee to knee in a cozy cafe with a band playing soft jazz in the background. While you drink a negroni I'd have a manhattan. You can tell me the story about each one of your tattoos.

Then when we had spent some time getting satisfyingly intrigued by each other, we'd go get to Smith & Wollensky's. While I drank my martini you could have lillet on the rocks. We can order a Petite Syrah to go with the steak and discuss the beauty of the universe. Once done I would let you win a game of billiards, after which I'd rescue "you from a gang of hoodlums.

Through the haze of my hangover the next morning I would wonder if it had all been a dream.

Hi :)

That sounds like the worst night of my life.

It's Not Just Me: Lauren (a different one), 29

I've dated all sorts of men: athletes, firefighters, pilots, politicians, comedians, writers, musicians, magicians, models, celebrities, restaurateurs, the list goes on. Let me get something straight though—I didn't sleep with all these people. I only dated them to see if we were a good match. And for the most part, we weren't, and I can't get those hours of my life back. Thanks a lot, Obama.

I have a theory that if I don't actively go out looking for people to date, I will meet someone organically. As a comedian, I have to follow one of the most important rules in improv: Don't force something to happen that wouldn't normally happen. I'm not on any dating sites, and I never leave my house thinking, *I'm gonna go hook up with someone tonight*. But I do leave my house thinking, *I will probably get hit by a SuperShuttle van and die today.*

I'm thirty, so most of my friends use Tinder and Match. I absolutely enjoy hearing their horror stories, but I really don't think the guy I want to be with is scrolling through Tinder or asking girls out over Twitter DM. I want to believe he's better than that. Of course, just because I do the dating thing "organically" doesn't mean it's any easier to find a quality guy.

This is a letter to my current self from my future self, to help me avoid ending up with horrible guys.

Dear Lauren, you idiot,

I know you really love this guy and you can totally see a future with him, but, honey, that's not gonna happen. You won't find this out until you're on vacation together, so let me just warn you right now: Homeslice is scared of everything. Stingrays, flying, boating, driving, you name it. He once drove two hours to your hotel at a pace no faster than fifteen miles per hour. This will be a major turnoff for you. If you guys ever had kids he would not be able to pick them up or drop them off. If both of your legs got eaten by a pack of wolves and you had to get to the hospital, he wouldn't be able to drive you. You'd have to wait for an ambulance like some sort of person who can afford to bleed out. Could you imagine being with someone so helpless?

I know you were used to dating athletes and strong guys, but this guy literally brags about never having worked out a day in his life. Plus, by being with someone who is totally inactive, you'll get fat with this person. But don't worry, you will take up smoking for a few months and lose a bunch of weight after the breakup.

This was almost a deal-breaker for you: You guys were in a kayak and it capsized in the ocean, and he didn't help pull the dumb boat all the way back to the hotel. YOU had to pull that thing through waves and brush more than a mile back while he pouted and held the oar. It was great exercise, but Jesus Christ, you can't be the man in this relationship.

You'll encounter some liars along the way, too. Here's a good one: One time you dated a guy who had his locks changed when you were out of town and made up a story that he sleepwalked into his hallway without a shirt on and had to hang out with his downstairs neighbors at seven in the morning till the locksmith arrived. Don't worry. You'll catch him lying and find out after the fact that he made the whole thing up; he just didn't want you to have keys anymore. Oh, this guy also hooks up with someone else, and you won't find that out till after the breakup, too. Don't worry, she's no Lauren.

Also, there's a person who literally stops sleeping with you nine months into your relationship because he suddenly finds you completely repulsive. It's okay; you're not (unless you count eating pizza for breakfast or drinking wine in bed repulsive).

There will come a point in one relationship when you think you really need this person; it's been a rough year and you were nothing but giving and honest. One day, out of the blue, he will end things and you will feel like you have absolutely nothing left to live for. You will be sad. You'll have to go on Xanax for the daily anxiety attacks and Ambien to put you to sleep every night. Don't worry though, Lauren. If there's one thing about you, it's that you're resilient. You will have an epiphany one day (it will feel like being struck by lightning), and suddenly, you won't hurt anymore.

I'm sure there's a guy out there for you who isn't afraid to live, is thoughtful, doesn't lie, and will only help you be a better person. Also, you will really enjoy being single again. I have some great stories about you—to avoid spoilers I won't get into it, but you'll see soon enough what I'm referring to.

Love,

Future Lauren

PS Still no flying cars in the future, WTF?!

Flash forward to the year 2020 for a follow-up: I'm still single.

The Thirty-Four-Year-Old Who "Just Isn't Ready"

A few months ago, I was camped on my couch watching a marathon of *Chopped* on the Food Network when a commercial for a new movie came on. I immediately started cracking up at the usual bullshit love-story plot. You know, the one where the classically gorgeous man and woman fall in love instantly upon locking eyes and exchanging witty banter—usually in some ridiculous context like spilling coffee on each other at their local coffee shop or dropping books on each other's feet at the cute little hole-in-the-wall indie bookstore. If the whole insta-passion-after-making-eye-contact thing was even slightly close to reality, the 579 attractive guys I see on the subway every day and I would've been married by now. We all know a more true-to-life modern romance would feature a thirty-four-year-old guy who "just doesn't want anything serious right now."

The night after I saw that commercial, I decided to break things off with Jeremy, the, yes, thirty-four-year-old guy I'd been seeing for over a month. He didn't know what he wanted—uh, except to have his cake and eat it, too. I'd been down that road before, and I knew it wouldn't end well.

Despite having recently disabled all my online dating profiles, Jeremy and I had met on Instagram, because apparently I can't escape the Internet. He was traveling when we first exchanged numbers, so we talked every day via FaceTime for about two weeks before meeting in person. It felt really natural—almost too good to be true—and we all know what they say when something seems too good to be true.

We texted almost all day, every day. I actually felt vulnerable with him—something that hadn't happened since Ethan, almost a year and a half before. Before I met Jeremy, I'd been this strong single woman who didn't want to date, well, pretty much anyone. Now here I was, letting my guard down and setting my schedule around a dude. Even though he could give me butterflies with something as simple as a fucking text message, the stress of my vulnerability and the possibility of getting hurt made me wish I was asexual.

After hanging out with Jeremy a few times and continuing to talk every day, things started to shift, and signs of the infamous thirty-four-year-old single-male stereotype started popping up. He was totally open to hanging out if I asked, but he wouldn't go out of his way to initiate plans. He also kept mentioning his exes and casually dropped that he wanted to "take things slow."

At first I thought I could deal with that, but I then I wondered what it even meant. What was the point of continuing to talk to this guy every day and get more and more emotionally invested if a month or two from now he'd just reiterate that he was still "just not ready for a girlfriend"? I wondered if he was looking only for a pen pal to cure his lonely nights, and the fact that I even wondered that made me think something wasn't right.

I can't say it didn't suck, though, because Jeremy was pretty much perfect aside from his mixed emotions. He was attractive, intelligent, genuine, honest, and whatever other positive adjectives you could possibly dream up. We had amazing chemistry, and he was extremely affectionate, always giving me a kiss or holding my hand when I least expected it. He also wasn't weird about introducing me to his friends. We aligned on so many levels . . . except the one where he actually felt like committing to me in any legitimate way. So I was pretty proud of myself when I cut things off, prioritizing my sanity over an ambivalent—but otherwise amazing—dude. I deserved someone who knew what he wanted (me, obviously).

Still, I wondered how many times I'd have to go through this shit with broken, single dudes between the ages of thirty-four and thirty-eight. It hadn't been my first go-round, of course. A year or so before Ethan, I'd gone through the same song and dance with Mark, a successful, thirty-eight-year-old salt-and-pepper-haired man I clicked with right away via text and over drinks. We spent a good ten hours together on our first date, talking about everything from mindless television to how fucked up our parents were, and despite our fifteen-year age difference, he drew me in with his confidence. After laughing over whiskey in slushie form and growing more and more excited by how much we'd clicked, I left our first date full of hope. Now I realize what I should've realized then: a single thirty-eight-year-old man is probably single for a good reason.

I saw Mark a couple more times, but all our interactions

came with tons of time in between. The more I got to know him, the more I sensed that he was a great dude who wanted to be independent, while simultaneously experiencing the occasional warm fuzzies of having a girl around to make out with. We're actually still friendly acquaintances, and I don't hold any bitter feelings toward him. He may have a bunch of great qualities, but holding down a monogamous relationship probably isn't one of them.

I'd like to thank Ethan for helping me realize when it's time to walk away from something that just isn't going to work. If it wasn't for that relationship, I would most likely *still* be letting Mark or Jeremy screw me around under the guise of "taking things slow." I'm all for not jumping into things rashly, but I'm not for moving at the pace of a handicapped snail. At a certain point, the relationship needs to grow and progress.

The issue with these kinds of dudes is that their desire to just "be independent" or "take things slow" usually comes at the expense of the women they're stringing along (er, sorry, "seeing"). They give them just enough encouraging signs to make the ladies think they'll come around, but what these guys really want is all the benefits of a relationship without the responsibility. And while I never got involved enough with Mark to get too deeply hurt, I did feel semi-shitty for a good few seconds after we parted ways.

I can't really compare Mark to Jeremy, though. They had similarities, sure, but I felt a much stronger connection with Jeremy. I honestly thought he was different and I guess that's why it was hard not to be a little bitter right after I let him go. It's like, awesome, so you're telling me that the first guy I've genuinely liked in over a year has way too much baggage to even think about attempting a relationship with me? Cool. Except it's not at all cool, and these situations just make me more and more frustrated and discouraged with men in general. I guess all I can do is move on, wait for the next guy to give my heart to, and hope he's stable enough to be ready for it.

The Types of Guys Who Message You on the Internet

Here are just a sampling of the specimens you may encounter when you date online.

The Bro

This guy usually has a healthy amount of shirtless selfies on his profile or Instagram. He usually opens his message with a "hey beautiful" or "sup girl?" Even better, he will say he likes your tats (if you have them), and you can assume that he's sending these messages to a minimum of ten other girls a day. Also, he's only looking to have sex with you even though you're most likely way out of his league.

The Passive-Aggressive Sexual Creep

This guy might seem normal at first, but after that message he sends you referring to you as his daughter, you realize he's a sick freakazoid.

The Very Blunt Nympho

This guy will not confuse you about what he wants. We can only assume he tried in the past to take the slow route of "wooing a girl" and failed, so he just gets right to the point now. He will tell you very specifically what he wants to do with your vagina before you even respond to his first message. He will give you graphic details, and you will most likely choke on that croissant you're eating. His message will wind up on They Really Said This.

The Headless Photo

This guy doesn't live in the same town as you—not even close, actually. He claims he doesn't want to put any photos of his face on his profile due to work, yet he will gladly send you photos if you ask. In the meantime, don't judge him on his shirtless photo that he has up. His message will be several paragraphs long, and he will claim he wants to worship you because you are clearly the love of his life. There will be endless winky faces in his profile, and typically in his what-he's-looking-for section, it simply says "you ;-)."

The Traveler

This guy is here only for the night, if you're lucky he's here for the week, but either way he wants to take you out for a drink and have some "fun." He'll most likely suggest an extremely touristy spot to go hang out at and act like you don't know anything about your own city.

The Nice Guy

This guy usually says all the right things, and while his profile might seem a bit bland, you're super close to going out with him just because you're sick of all the headless, shirtless bodies messaging you. He's not bad looking, he even has a puppy, but you're not actually attracted to him. You know what's really making him look good to you is the golden retriever and the contrast between him and the other douches.

The Guy Who States an Overly Obvious Fact
Your profile might state that you like food, and he will send a message telling you to check out bacon.

The Exception
Whoa, is this guy real? Have you found someone who seems normal and genuine and is attractive? He might seem too good to be true, and you may find out in the future he is, but for now he's at least worth a first date. Congrats on navigating the guys who message you on the Internet!

Options, Options, and More Options

A s I walked through the endless rows of self-serve food options at Whole Foods this afternoon, I had to consciously ask myself—and keep asking myself over and over—what I wanted to eat for lunch. It was cold outside, so I knew I wanted something warm. Should I get the soup? The spicy Thai shrimp thing? Wait a sec. Then I remembered that I'm trying to eat healthy right now (ugh), so I'd need to ignore all the delectable-looking fried/pasta/red-meat options. That left me with fifteen choices or so, which is, obviously, still too damn many. Perplexed and slightly overwhelmed by all the mental energy I'd just expended on selecting a meal that would take me less than fifteen minutes to finish and forget, I settled for warm veggies, risotto, and baked chicken.

I've started to wonder more than ever if having too many dating options is like having too many self-serve choices at Whole Foods. I think I might be on to something, because back in 2000, there was a study that examined people's buying habits. Researchers asked customers to participate in a tasting of different kinds of jam. The researchers offered a choice of six different jams on the first day and twenty-four jams the next. When offered six jams, about 30 percent of samplers purchased a jar. When faced with twenty-four choices, though, only 3 percent bought a jar.

That study perfectly illustrates my point: When given too many choices, we imbecile humans become too indecisive. Then we tend to either get paralyzed and not make a decision at all, get all unsure and paranoid about whether we're making the right one, or we obsess after the fact about whether we've now missed out on something "better."

Author Barry Schwartz wrote about this phenomenon in his book *The Paradox of Choice*. Schwartz outlines how having too many possibilities in any area of life can actually make people miserable—overrun with regret, fear, and the deluded sense that "only the best will do." Is this the real reason so many of us are single? I mean, of course there'll always be that lame slacker dude who's terrified of commitment and the tear-streaked pinot grigio–chugging girl who's still hung up on her ex, but aside from them, in a world full of choices, do we simply have too many to ever feel ready to calmly focus on *one*?

And perhaps more importantly for the purposes of this book, how can we use the Internet to date without driving ourselves batshit insane worrying about whether to bother replying to this one or that one or the other one? Well, one thing to try, before diving headfirst into the thousands of dating options that seem so majestically laid out before you online, is to sit down and establish what your top requirements are when it comes to potential matches. Deal-breakers can be good; they can help you refine what you're looking for. The key is to not have so many of them that you start limiting your potential pool to *only* floppy-haired brunettes within five miles of your house who speak Portuguese, are over six foot two, and make more than $150,000.

A couple of my biggest deal-breakers are smoking and religion (like, dude can't be even a tiny bit "of God"). This obviously cuts a bunch of men from my pool, but it narrows it down to people I'd actually consider going out with. Like I said, though, being TOO picky is useless, and analyzing your matches' responses to every petty, dumb-ass compatibility question won't get you any closer to finding a good one. "Would it bother you if your significant other felt very uncomfortable in 'dress-up' clothes and preferred jeans and T-shirts most of the time?" should not be the determining factor in who *anybody* goes out with.

Another issue when it comes to this stuff is that having what seems like a constantly refilled stream of options falsely lulls people into believing that they, well, have a constantly refilled stream of options. Because, honestly? They don't. All the clicking, swiping, and insta-judging just starts to feel dehumanizing, like you're assessing someone's potential as a partner based only on looks (i.e., on bullshit).

The depressing attitude that people are disposable when it comes to online dating, that there's always a potentially better match waiting just beyond the next thumb swipe, has only worsened since I started doing this several years ago. I used to be excited to go on dates. (Can you *imagine*?!) If a smart, cute, sane-seeming dude and I started a promising conversation online, we'd most likely meet up, and I'd most likely be psyched about it. Now I'd rather hang at home or even work late than get a drink with someone I'm not 100 percent sure is going to be a good time.

Therein lies the problem. Internet dating fuels this troubling norm where we're all sitting around mindlessly making snap judgments about people we actually might have stellar in-person chemistry with. If we'd only actually take the time—and the risk—to step away from Netflix and meet them face-to-face.

But limiting your time browsing online can help slow down all those snap judgments. Recently, I stopped checking dating sites more than once a day, if that. It can really help prevent you from falling into a weird obsessive spiral about the whole thing, which lots of people do, and remember that the rest of your life is actually far more important than some rando you were talking to on Tinder yesterday.

I also try to chill for a minute when I *do* find someone I like. For example, if I go on a first date with "Matt" and find him attractive, witty, and free of grammatical ineptitude, I'll stop obsessively checking OKCupid looking for other guys until I've given things with Matt a fair shot. Other people may think that slows down the game a bit too much, but what's the rush? What if jumping right back into messaging a bunch of other men the night after your date with Matt distracts you to the point of missing a message from him, which leads to you never seeing him again, which leads to you potentially never hooking up with the guy who could have been the love of your life? (Sorry, not trying to use scare tactics, just trying to prove a point.) Giving a sliver of attention to one hundred guys feels so much emptier and less satisfying than giving a legit chunk of attention to one. Even if they don't turn out to be the person you end up with, hey, at least you checked it out.

Another thing that can help take some of the insane pressure off when it comes to option overload is to always go with your gut when it comes to this stuff. Like I discuss on page 108, I honestly believe that when it comes to dating, your intuition is never wrong. If a flashing CREEP ALERT rings in your brain when you first notice the profile of a man who looks OMG-SO-FUCKING-PERFECT in his pictures, don't trust the pictures! They're pictures. He might be thirty years older and forty pounds fatter in real life. Believe me: Trust the creep alert. This will help you instantly narrow down your choices—it'll also help you avoid some totally unnecessary future heartache.

It's Not Just Me: Nikki

HIM: I wanna do voiceover work. How does one get their foot in the door.

ME: Are you being serious? Or fucking with me?

HIM: Serious. I watched *In a World* last year. Seems like an interesting job. I would say go watch my clips online, but I don't think the recording justify my range. I recorded this killer set my last night in Boston. If you give me your email, I'll send you my set from Boston it's pretty funny. It's just a recording. Audio. If you watch my videos my Youtube one was a year and half ago and I've lost weight. Everything else was when I was really young. Like rooftop.

ME: No, thank you. This is exactly why I don't ever tell anyone where I work. Best of luck. Bye.

HIM: It's cool. I'm sorry. I ruined it. Was it my material? Bc I don't say touch of Down syndrome anymore. I say it looks like he was born with 5 concussions . . . I don't care if you don't wanna work with me. I'm totally ok with you telling me my voice isn't voiceover friendly. We can still get together. But I'm funny. I open for Kevin Nealon, I was a finalist in Funniest Person in Austin, and I was 1 of 98 to go to the Boston Comedy Festival. I don't need your job but I might want your company. But huge apology for asking, that was rude. It was the material, huh? A lot of that's old old old if you'd just listen to my set Saturday.

HIM [later]: Hey I know you don't owe me anything, but I'd much appreciate some constructive criticism. You can be as mean as you want, just tell me why you hate me all of a sudden. I honestly don't care. I swear I'll erase your number and delete you from my Tinder. Just tell me why you think I'm not good enough. It might help me grow as an entertainer.

HIM [even later]: Fine. Bye. I don't want your opinion anyway.

Hey Lauren, I'm Chris

I'm a cartoonist

How's your weekend going Lauren? Any big plans?

your tatts are so great, especially the moon on your finger ~

think it'd be really fun to see you some time . . . wondering about us

Such a crazy week, so relieved that I can finally untense . . . L how have you been doing? been so looking forward to relaxing at Bell House by watching some Eliot Glazer this week, if you're at all any curious I would love to take you?

What I've Learned from Endless Amounts of Online Dating

Someone can seem absolutely perfect in their photos and texts, but you can end up having absolutely zero chemistry in person.

Last summer, I decided to meet up with a guy I came across on Happn. I can't say I wasn't skeptical—by then I'd had my fair share of disappointing dates—but his pictures were fine, meaning there was a close-up of his face, there were no group shots of guys holding Bud Lights, and there was a lack of laughable snaps where he donned sunglasses while standing in front of a national landmark grinning like some kind of mythic conqueror. (My friend Jeremy almost started a Tumblr that would solely contain Internet-dating photos of people at Machu Picchu, because this trend is actually getting quite comical and out of hand.)

Anyway, my date, Josh, looked good, and after chatting with him via text, he seemed intelligent to boot. We planned a date on a beautiful day in Brooklyn's Prospect Park (*worlds* better than Central Park, but of course). He told me he would pick up food, drinks, even a picnic blanket. I was pleasantly taken aback that he was going out of his way to do all that for someone he really didn't know at all—it was 2014, not 1957. I started to actually *get excited* for this date, and me getting excited for a date is as rare as a cat giving a flying fuck when you command it to get off your countertop (or do anything else, for that matter).

Then I saw him walking toward me in the park. The second he opened his mouth, I knew it wasn't gonna work. It wasn't his voice or what he *said*, exactly. It was just . . . you might not *always* instantly know whether the spark is there right away, but you *do* know if the spark is, like, the absolute literal opposite of there right away.

As we perched on his blanket and did the ostensibly cute alfresco thing, he talked about himself constantly while heaving Brie into his face. His gut overflowing out of his shirt only added to the hotness of this, and he didn't bother to pull it down even once. After more cheese shoveling and more bragging about how much exotic world travel he'd done that year, he glanced down at his phone and noted, "I actually need to get going soon."

I quickly agreed that I had "so much to do," and that vaguely awkward silent understanding that we both totally weren't into each other passed between us. Naturally, we never spoke (er, texted) again, which was A-OK by me.

People Can Pull a 180 Personality Flip When You Least Expect It

One of the strangest online dating experiences I've ever had went down a couple weeks before my birthday last summer. As you've most certainly learned by now, I've gone on a ton of unsuccessful first dates, and thus I rarely remember their names (about 80 percent of them are called Mike or Chris anyway). For the sake of the story, let's call this winner Steven.

Steven and I were getting along almost too well for the first couple hours of our date at an East Village bar. He was covered in tattoos and looked very put together. It felt really natural, like we had been seeing each other for longer than um, less than one date. After a while we moved to another bar, and he asked if it was okay if his cousin joined us. I was dubious. It seemed a little bizarre to let another dude tag along on your date, but he said he was only asking because his cousin was new to the city and had time to kill. Said "cousin" showed up and was a skeezy-looking, skinny European dandy wearing a sheer pink button-up and pleated black dress pants. That's when shit started to get *real* weird.

Drinks were flowing, and soon Steven's personality started to change. While it may have been kind of amusing—even slightly flattering—the first time he'd said it, he started referring to me as his fiancée to his cousin and to strangers around us. He started obsessing over everything I did and complimenting me every other sentence. It was the first time I'd seen a dude get extremely vulnerable on a first date and tell me about how badly he wanted to find the love of his life to settle down and have kids with. It was desperate, unappealing, and crystal clear that he was trying to force a relationship down any female's throat without even bothering to get to know her. He stepped away from the table to go to the bathroom and actually *texted me from there.*

I know, I know. Obvious psychopath. But don't judge me for sticking around—I was semi-drunk and therefore willing to tolerate much more than I would have sober. Plus, I knew this experience would turn into a great story. (I was right, right?)

The three of us hopped in a cab and Steven launched into a heated argument with the driver about an obscure country in Asia. I jumped in and broke up the argument as Steven's creep cousin just sat there dumbly in his see-through shirt. The whole point of leaving the last bar was to find something to eat, and they decided, as we were in the cab, that Benihana's would be PERFECT. Each new turn of events just became more ridiculous than the last, so I felt like I *had* to tag along to this classy establishment where food was thrown casually at your face.

Steven started telling everyone at our communal, tourist-stuffed Benihana table that we were engaged, which I pretty much laughed off without confirming or denying. He bought the whole table mai tais and several bottles of sake. I don't know exactly why mai tais were one of Benihana's "signature cocktails" since they obvs have no Japanese connection whatsoever, but maybe I shouldn't expect authenticity from a cheesy, generic chain restaurant.

With a full mouth of delicious fried rice, we'd almost made it through dinner when Steven turned to me and sternly said, "This isn't going to work."

"Ummm, what are you talking about?" I asked.

He continued to mumble, seeming to have a legit conversation with the split personalities battling it out in his head. He then accused me of "sabotaging our love," saying I wasn't paying attention to him, that it seemed like I actually wanted to date the tourist girl I'd been politely chatting with.

NO WORDS.

Then Steven abruptly called the waitress over and asked for

the bill, demanding that I pay half of it. I laughed; I would never have agreed to hit up an overpriced chain near Times Square if I knew I'd be paying, and it certainly hadn't been *my* decision to pass out free drinks to old Swedish ladies.

With food still on our plates and the tourists just as confused as I was, Steven stood and theatrically walked out after paying a portion of the check. His cousin followed. I sat there for a good five minutes finishing my food, because duh.

When I got to the bottom of the stairs on my way out, I found Steven waiting. The look on his face was that of a guilty dude who had cheated on his wife. He lunged toward me. "I'm so sorry," he pleaded. "I just really want this—us—to be perfect, so we can spend the rest of our lives together."

My expression could easily have been described as that emoji with its eyes bugged out. I hightailed it out of that restaurant as fast as I could and headed for the train. Steven followed me for two blocks, begging for forgiveness. Once he'd finally stopped following me, he yelled down the street, "ARE YOU SURE THIS IS WHAT YOU WANT?!" Um, dude—I had never been so sure about anything in my life.

People Will Sacrifice Hours of Their Lives, Bored out of Their Minds on Bad Dates, in an Attempt Not to Offend Someone

I can't tell you how many times I've gone out with someone and knew, within the first thirty seconds, that it just wasn't going to click. That doesn't mean I left, however. Nope, I almost always stick around for an hour or two because leaving feels uncouth and, well, mean. What am I supposed to say? "Hey, so ummmm,

I know I actually know nothing about you, but your voice/shoes/ breath/teeth just aren't working for me."

Still, though, when I finally do say goodbye, I make a point of being honest about how I feel, because I'd rather someone just tell me they don't think it'll work out than give me BS hope for a second date. Of course that's happened to me plenty of times. ("I'll text you," they mutter, as their eyes say something else). Who the fuck knows, maybe I wasn't as skinny or ladylike as they expected? Anyway, as Dita Von Teese says, "You can be the ripest, juiciest peach in the world, and there's still going to be someone who hates peaches."

Herein lies one of the biggest problems with meeting people online: The only information you have about them are the messages they write and the photos they provide. It's an ideal example of how someone can be perfect on paper (or onscreen), but be utterly incompatible with you face-to-face. It's impossible not to put a lot of pressure on those first thirty seconds of meeting. If the very first moments are disappointing, you're in for at least an hour of forced conversation, and if you leave before that hour, you're considered an asshole. You can't win.

You Never Know Who You'll Meet

I follow lots of scientists on social media. I like keeping up with whatever the cool new discovery is, and I obsessively devour obscure facts about the universe. I'd freak out more if I had the chance to meet Carl Sagan over Justin Timberlake any day.

One night I was scrolling through Twitter when Bill Nye the Science Guy retweeted a photo of himself with Jay-Z. I started following Brandon, the guy who'd posted the original photo of the dynamic duo, and over the next few weeks, I tweeted back and forth with him here and there. Eventually, he asked if I wanted to grab a drink sometime.

We went on a couple of dates and actually got along pretty well. On our third outing, after an amazing dinner, he asked if I was up for heading to a bar. "I have a surprise for you," he said.

When we got to the spot, as Brandon was speaking to the hostess, Bill Nye-the-mother-fucking-Science Guy walked in and made eye contact with me. I was internally trying not to completely lose my shit, but somehow managed to introduce myself and shake his hand. Brandon was actually a good friend of Bill's, and *that* was my surprise.

I would have never anticipated that following some random on Twitter would lead to me shooting the shit while drinking whiskey with one of my heroes for a couple hours on a Tuesday. And though Brandon and I didn't pan out—we weren't looking for the same thing—I am forever indebted to him for facilitating a hangout with someone I respect so much, and it's not lost on me that I never would have experienced it if it weren't for the weird, occasional wonder of meeting dudes on the Internet.

The Day Things Changed

F or the most part, we go through our days with very particular expectations—what time we'll get home, what we'll
watch on TV that night, all the thrilling minutiae that makes
up our everyday existences. On the same tip, I, like anyone else,
would be shocked if, on any given Tuesday, someone handed me
fifty thousand dollars on the street, or David Beckham casually
strode up and asked me out for drinks.

January 20, 2014, was no exception. (Though, side note: I
actually did wind up standing in the right place at the right time
about nine months later. David Beckham did, in fact, casually
walk right past me, but sadly no date.)

Anyway, it was shitty and cold outside and I had just gotten
dumped by Ethan a month earlier. Still getting over a breakup
that completely blindsided me, I was working in retail, dragging
miserably through my day, when I took my lunch break. I checked
my phone approximately five thousand times, as usual, and after
deleting the twenty-third email that week from Crate & Barrel,

I opened an email from a woman named Ashley from OKCupid. She wanted to know if it was OK for her to pass along my contact info to a publication writing an article about the site. The email was vague, but I agreed and got on with my less-than-stellar day. Little did I know that publication was *New York* magazine and that I'd just been crowned the most-messaged straight female on one of the most popular dating sites in the world.

It fascinates me that we never know what might result from some seemingly small, petty happening in our lives. If I'd just skimmed past that email from Ashley like the rest of the junk I receive, I wouldn't be writing this right now. I wouldn't have believed you if you'd told me *Buzzfeed*, the *Daily Mail*, even some random fucking Malaysian newspaper would soon be splashing my photo across their sites for all the world to see, or that I'd be doing a bunch of radio interviews for stations across the country, or that I'd be contacted by tons of production companies wanting to air my life on television.

Lots of people ask, "So, like, what happened after the article and stuff?" I don't have a straightforward answer. Yeah, I wrote this book and I gained a few followers on Instagram, but the main thing that occurs to me is how much my views on life have changed. While being chosen for the *New York* piece was half luck and half whatever else, I'm thrilled that I got so lucky—I wouldn't change the experience for anything. Though I didn't quite know how to handle it emotionally, I think crawling out of your comfort zone is the only way to grow. The experience has helped me hone in on who I really am, what makes me happy, and what I want. And perhaps most importantly, I've become more sensitive to what other people around me might be going through.

You may wonder how a completely complimentary, ego-boosting article could lead to me becoming more attuned to other people. Well, you try reading a pages-long comment section entirely devoted to your appearance—let me assure you, it's pretty much the most humbling thing, ever. "Humbling" might be a little too kind a word, actually. It can be the most self-esteem-annihilating process of your life if not handled properly. People are fucking mean, and I'm not even famous. I completely understand why Britney shaved her head in 2007—shout-out to her for handling that drama *sans* drug overdose or worse. How anyone put through that much criticism stays sane is a mystery to me. Besides the comments on articles (which I stopped reading), I started receiving a mass influx of messages on Facebook, Twitter, Tumblr, and via email, all from strangers.

Many of them made assumptions about me, bashing me for countless things they knew nothing about. I mean, the only information they had about me was from articles written by people who'd never met me. At first I would tweet back or respond to the losers who called me a tramp, cunt, blah blah blah. Then I realized it didn't matter how I responded, because there would always be an asshole with nothing better to do than troll on the Internet. In that respect, dealing with constant criticism from thousands of people made me stronger and more carefree when it comes to what everyone else thinks. Now, if someone came up to me and said, "Oh, I hear *insert celebrity name here* is a total bitch," I'd most likely tell them that they've never met said person, so they have no right to presume that. It makes me sick reading comments under celebrities' Instagram photos. It's almost funny (ALMOST funny, not actually funny) how much people believe everything they read. Also, why the fuck do people *care*?

Besides being flooded with negative crap, I received plenty of messages along the lines of "hey how r u, love your tats, can I take u out" from guys who completely disregarded anything I was actually interested in. I also got a lot of insightful messages like, "Oh, aren't you the most popular girl on OKCupid?" Of course there were a few normals, too, but . . . well, not really.

I stayed on OKC, but scaled back the number of dates I went on. I didn't really know what I wanted. I think I initially joined the site again because I was freshly dumped, and what better way to cure a broken heart than via brand-new specimens?

I've probably gone on more first dates than the average woman my age, but I thought all the boring, bizarre, frighteningly awkward interactions HAD to end at some point (they do, right?), so I kept trying. Some people may have called me a serial dater, but I definitely didn't *enjoy* it or anything. I would have been much more content getting really high and staring at my fucking cat.

After the *New York* story came out, I remember going out with this guy, Bobby, a couple of times. It's rare to get past a first date in NYC, so the fact that we were going on a second was kind of a big deal. He'd never mentioned the article or being aware of my growing Internet presence, so I didn't bother to bring it up. At the end of our second date he casually informed me that he had actually read my whole blog and tons of articles about me; he had been asking me questions he already knew the answers to.

That's when I realized my dating life was going to change. I don't feel special or intimidating just because of all that media crap, but when a guy Googles you before your date and comes across tons of press on the Most Popular Girl on OKCupid, it can make things . . . peculiar. It tends to go one of two ways: Either they see me as a challenge and just want to go out with me so they can say they did afterward. Or they're scared off by the amount of extremely superficial information out there about me, and assume I have no substance.

Over the last year I've fluctuated between phases of wanting to be single and wanting a solid relationship. The times I crave a boy-friend are mostly at night when I'm home alone, or when something really cool happens and I want to tell someone about it. Currently my friend Alison fills the position of Someone I Can Text Who Will Always Respond, and I'm lucky to have that (even if it's just to describe the crazy adorable golden retriever I just walked past). Being single mostly works for me, though. Work keeps me extremely busy, and I fear that even if I met someone great, I'd just end up pulling away because I love my independence so much.

Since receiving the extra attention, my blog has gained a large number of loyal followers. The whole time I was receiving all those negative messages and desperate come-ons, I was also getting thank-yous and cool personal stories from tons of people, which helped me realize that I could actually use the attention for a good cause. It feels great hearing that I've inspired women, whether it be to try online dating for the first time or even to get out of an abusive relationship.

The last year has done wonders for me, and I'm excited to see what will evolve from it. The next guy I start a serious relation-ship with will need to be as driven, passionate, and confident as I am in order to deal with my absurd schedule and all my ambitious future plans.

I'd like to thank a few people. Thanks to all the nice guys, douches, and obnoxious men that made these stories possible. Jess Regel for thinking my life is actually interesting. Alison with one L. Kathleen, my Czech sister. And finally, every dog that has ever crossed my path.

Lauren Urasek is a science enthusiast turned make-up artist in her mid-twenties. After being inundated with online dating messages, she began to document them in her popular Tumblr, theyreallysaidthis.com. When she's not making fun of ridiculous online dating messages, she's painting the faces of celebrities, and most likely becoming best friends with your dog. You can follow her on Twitter and Instagram @LoandtheCosmos.

Laura Barcella is a writer, editor, feminist, candy junkie, crime nerd, animal nut, and reluctant Internet-dating pro. She's the author of *The End: 50 Apocalyptic Visions From Pop Culture That You Should Know About . . . Before It's Too Late*, and the editor of *Madonna & Me: Women Writers On The Queen Of Pop*. She's also written for approximately 618 magazines and websites, some of which you may have actually read. Visit her website at laurabarcella. com, and follow her on Twitter @laurabarcella and Instagram @laurabarcella1.